Taxcafe.co.uk Tax Guides

Furnished Holiday Lets

Your Emergency Tax Planning Guide

By Carl Bayley BSc ACA

Important Legal Notices:

Taxcafe®
TAX GUIDE – "Furnished Holiday Lets – Your Emergency Tax Planning Guide"

Published by:
Taxcafe UK Limited
67 Milton Road
Kirkcaldy
KY1 1TL
United Kingdom
Tel: (01592) 560081

First Edition, October 2009
Second Edition, January 2010

ISBN 978-1-907302-06-0

Disclaimer
Before reading or relying on the content of this Tax Guide, please read carefully the disclaimer on the last page which applies. If you have queries then please contact the publisher at team@taxcafe.co.uk.

About the Author

Carl Bayley is the author of a series of 'Plain English' tax guides designed specifically for the layman. Carl's particular speciality is his ability to take the weird, complex and inexplicable world of taxation and set it out in the kind of clear, straightforward language that taxpayers themselves can understand. As he often says himself, "my job is to translate 'tax' into English".

Carl enjoys his role as a tax author, as he explains: "Writing these guides gives me the opportunity to use the skills and knowledge learned over almost twenty-five years in the tax profession for the benefit of a wider audience. The most satisfying part of my success as an author is the chance to give the average person the same standard of advice as the 'big guys' at a price which everyone can afford."

Carl takes the same approach when speaking on taxation, a role he frequently undertakes with great enthusiasm, including his highly acclaimed annual 'Budget Breakfast' for the Institute of Chartered Accountants.

In addition to being a recognised author and speaker on the subject, Carl has often spoken on property taxation on radio and television, including the BBC's 'It's Your Money' programme and BBC Radio 2's Jeremy Vine Show.

Carl began his career as a Chartered Accountant in 1983 with one of the 'Big 4' accountancy firms. After qualifying as a double prize-winner, he immediately began specialising in taxation.

After honing his skills with several major international firms, Carl began the new millennium by launching his own tax and accounting practice, Bayley Miller Limited, through which he provides advice on a wide variety of taxation issues; especially property taxation, Inheritance Tax and tax planning for small and medium-sized businesses.

Carl is a member of the governing Council of the Institute of Chartered Accountants in England and Wales and a former Chairman of the Institute Members in Scotland group. He has co-organised the annual Peebles Tax Conference for the last eight years.

When he isn't working, Carl takes on the equally taxing challenges of hill walking and writing poetry and fiction. Carl lives in Scotland with his partner Isabel and has four children.

Dedication

For the Past,

Firstly, I dedicate this book to the memory of those I have loved and lost:

First of all, to my beloved mother Diana – what would you think if you could see me now? The memory of your love warms me still. Thank you for making it all possible;

To my dear grandfather, Arthur - your wise words still come back to guide me; and to my loving grandmothers, Doris and Winifred;

Between you, you left me with nothing I could spend, but everything I need.

Also to my beloved friend and companion, Dawson, who waited so patiently for me to come home every night and who left me in the middle of our last walk together. Thank you for all those happy miles; I still miss you son.

For the Present,

Above all, I must dedicate this book to the person who stands, like a shining beacon, at the centre of every part of my life: Isabel, my 'life support system', whose unflinching support has seen me through the best and the worst. Whether anyone will ever call me a 'great man' I do not know, but I do know that I have a great woman behind me.

Without her help, support and encouragement, this book, and the others I have written, could never have been.

For the Future,

Finally, I also dedicate this book to four very special young people: Michelle, Louise, James and Robert.

I am so very proud of every one of you and I can only hope that I, in turn, will also be able to leave each of you with everything that you need.

Thanks

First and foremost, I must say an enormous thank you to Isabel: for all her help researching everything from obscure points of tax legislation to popular girls' names in Asia; for reading countless drafts; for making sure I stop to eat and sleep; for putting up with me when I'm under pressure and, most of all, for keeping me company into the 'wee small hours' on many a long and otherwise lonely night. I simply cannot ever thank her enough for everything that she does for me, but I intend to spend the rest of my life trying!

The next biggest thanks have to go to my good friend, colleague and 'comrade-in-arms', Nick, who believed in me long before I did. Thanks for keeping the faith mate.

Thanks to the rest of the Taxcafe team, past and present, for their help in making these books far more successful than I could ever have dreamed.

I would like to thank my old friend and mentor, Peter Rayney, for his inspiration and for showing me that tax and humour can mix.

And last, but far from least, thanks to Ann for keeping us right!

C.B., Roxburghshire, January 2010

BUSINESS TAX SAVER

If you like this tax guide...

You will also like *Business Tax Saver*...

Our monthly guide to BIG business tax savings

<u>You can try it for just £1</u>

Go to www.taxcafe.co.uk/businesstaxsaver.html

Contents

Contents

Contents

Introduction

For many years, furnished holiday lettings have enjoyed the best of all worlds. In effect, they are treated as investment properties whenever that is more beneficial, but get treated like a normal trading business whenever most trading reliefs are up for grabs.

They can sometimes qualify as private residential accommodation and yet still get so many of the advantages generally reserved for commercial property. Until now, getting a property to qualify as furnished holiday accommodation has been the property tax equivalent of winning the lottery!

Sadly, all this is about to come to an end, as the Government proposes to abolish the furnished holiday letting regime with effect from 6th April 2010.

The announcement of the impending abolition of the furnished holiday letting regime in the Budget on 22nd April 2009 provided landlords with little more than eleven months' notice and came as quite a shock to the holiday rental sector.

The abolition of the regime will fundamentally alter the tax position of thousands of landlords and yet the Government did not provide any details of how the change will be handled until the Pre-Budget Report on 9th December 2009: leaving holiday letting landlords to 'wait and wonder' for almost eight months!

Throughout this eight month period, many questions were being asked but going unanswered by the Government. Questions like 'How will holiday lettings be treated in future?', 'Will everyone be treated the same?' and 'What will the transitional rules to deal with the change be like?'

Finally, with the publication of the detailed transitional rules on 9th December 2009, we can begin to answer these questions.

It must be admitted, however, that a few areas of uncertainty do still remain. For one thing, the transitional rules are only in draft and the final version may not become law until **after** the furnished holiday letting regime has been abolished.

Some aspects of the transition are also open to a great deal of interpretation: especially the issue of what constitutes a trading business (see Chapter 8). It may be many years before a definitive view emerges in court.

What follows in this guide is therefore based on the transitional rules as they currently stand and on existing case law. Although we may see some changes in the months and years ahead, this must be the best basis on which furnished holiday letting landlords can plan their affairs.

Many important tax reliefs are currently available on furnished holiday letting properties and it is vital for landlords to consider action **now** in order to reap the benefit of these reliefs before the abolition of the regime on 6th April 2010.

In this guide I am therefore going to show you precisely which tax reliefs are going to be taken away from furnished holiday lettings, what you can do about it before it's too late and just how much tax you might save by taking the right steps.

I will begin by providing a brief recap of the current furnished holiday letting regime and its advantages.

I will then proceed to look in detail at the planning opportunities between now and 5th April 2010 by examining each of the main tax reliefs currently available in turn and considering what action can be taken to maximise the value of those reliefs before the regime is abolished.

As we consider each of the main tax reliefs currently available, I will also guide you through the potential future tax landscape for furnished holiday lettings after 6th April 2010. This tour of the future will end with a look at a possible escape route in Chapter 8, where I will consider the possibility that some furnished holiday letting businesses might become trading businesses.

Chapter 9 then covers some important additional points which need to be considered when undertaking any of the planning outlined in this guide.

Finally, in Chapter 10 at the end of the guide, I will also look at the recent extension of the furnished holiday letting regime to the European Economic Area.

Scope of this Guide

Both the impending abolition of the furnished holiday letting regime and its recent extension to property throughout the European Economic Area apply to all business entities, including companies. In this guide, however, we will mainly concentrate on unincorporated furnished holiday letting businesses run by individuals or partnerships, as these are more common.

This guide is also aimed primarily at UK resident landlords owning furnished holiday letting property in the UK or elsewhere in the European Economic Area (see Appendix B).

This guide deals only with the UK tax consequences of investing in furnished holiday lettings. Foreign taxation is beyond its scope.

For tax purposes, the UK does not include the Channel Islands or the Isle of Man, but comprises only England, Scotland, Wales and Northern Ireland.

Wealth Warning

It is important to remember that both UK residents investing in property overseas and non-UK residents investing in UK property may also face foreign tax liabilities on their property income and capital gains. Each country has its own tax system, and income or gains which are exempt in the UK may nevertheless still be liable to tax elsewhere.

Additionally, in some cases, citizens of another country who are resident in the UK for tax purposes may nevertheless still have obligations and liabilities under their own country's tax system. The USA, for example, imposes this type of obligation on its expatriate citizens.

It is only when talking about taxpayers who are both UK residents and UK citizens, and who are investing exclusively in UK property, that we can be absolutely certain that no other country has any right to tax the income or gains arising.

More detailed information on the taxation issues encountered when investing in property overseas, including foreign taxation, is provided in the Taxcafe.co.uk guide *'How to Avoid Tax on Foreign Property'*.

Finally, the reader must bear in mind the general nature of this guide. Individual circumstances vary and the tax implications of an individual's actions will vary with them. For this reason, it is always vital to get professional advice before undertaking any tax planning or other transactions which may have tax implications. The author cannot accept any responsibility for any loss which may arise as a consequence of any action taken, or any decision to refrain from action taken, as a result of reading this guide.

A Word about the Examples in this Guide

This guide is illustrated throughout by a number of examples.

Unless specifically stated to the contrary, all persons described in the examples in this guide are UK resident, ordinarily resident and domiciled for tax purposes.

In preparing the examples in this guide, we have assumed that the UK tax regime will remain unchanged in the future except to the extent of any announcements already made at the time of publication, including the Pre-Budget Report on 9th December 2009.

Whilst it is probable that proposals announced to date will become law, it is nevertheless worth bearing in mind that some of these proposals are not yet law and may undergo some alteration before they are formally enacted.

If there is one thing which we can predict with any certainty it is the fact that change **will** occur. The reader must bear this in mind when reviewing the results of our examples.

All persons described in the examples in this guide are entirely fictional characters created specifically for the purposes of this guide. Any similarities to actual persons, living or dead, or to fictional characters created by any other author, are entirely coincidental.

Chapter 1

The Current Regime

1.1 QUALIFYING PROPERTIES

To begin our look at furnished holiday lettings, we need to consider what properties actually qualify under the current regime.

The qualification requirements for a property to be regarded as a furnished holiday letting are as follows:

i) The property must be situated in the European Economic Area (see Appendix B).
ii) The property must be furnished (to at least the minimum level which an occupier would usually expect).
iii) It must be let out on a commercial basis with a view to the realisation of profits.
iv) It must be available for commercial letting to the public generally for at least 140 days in a 12-month period.
v) It must be so let for at least 70 such days.
vi) The property must not normally be in the same occupation for more than 31 consecutive days at any time during a period of at least seven months out of the same 12-month period as that referred to in (iv) above. This seven month period need not be a single continuous period but must include the lettings under (v) above.

The 12-month period referred to in (iv) and (vi) above is normally the UK tax year (see Section 1.4), but see Section 9.1 regarding newly acquired property. A taxpayer with more than one furnished holiday letting property may use a system of averaging to determine whether they meet test (v).

Whilst the property need not be in a recognised holiday area, the lettings should strictly be to holidaymakers and tourists in order to qualify.

Where a property qualifies, as set out above, then it generally qualifies for the whole of each qualifying tax year, subject to special rules for the years in which holiday letting commences or ceases.

1.2 THE BENEFITS OF FURNISHED HOLIDAY LETTINGS

In essence, properties qualifying as 'furnished holiday lettings' enjoy a special tax regime, which includes many of the tax advantages usually only accorded to trading properties.

At the same time, however, the profits derived from furnished holiday lettings are still treated as rental income.

We will be exploring each of the available reliefs listed below in more detail later in the guide, when I will also explain all of the terminology used in this section.

The current taxation benefits of qualifying furnished holiday lettings include the following:

Capital Gains Tax

- Entrepreneurs' relief.
- Rollover relief on replacement of business assets.
- Holdover relief for gifts.
- Incorporation relief.
- Relief for 'loans to traders'.

Income Tax/Corporation Tax

- Capital allowances for furniture and equipment, fixtures and fittings and integral features.
- Losses may be set off against other income of the same tax year or the previous one.
- Losses arising in 2008/9 or 2009/10 may also be carried back for set off against furnished holiday letting profits from the same business in the previous three years (with a £50,000 limit on losses arising in each year carried back more than a year).
- Furnished holiday letting profits are qualifying 'earnings' for pension contribution purposes.

And Yet ...

- Despite its 'trading-style' advantages, National Insurance should not usually be payable in respect of income from furnished holiday accommodation (although some local tax offices do insist on collecting Class 2 contributions at £2.40 per week).
- A non-UK resident investing in UK furnished holiday accommodation would usually continue to be exempt from Capital Gains Tax.

A furnished holiday letting business may also be exempt from Inheritance Tax where the lettings are generally short-term (e.g. weekly or fortnightly) and the owner (or their agents or employees) is substantially involved with the holidaymakers' activities.

The available reliefs extend to any property used in a furnished holiday letting business. This will include not only the holiday accommodation itself but also any office premises from which the business is run.

Where there is some other use of the property, some of the Capital Gains Tax reliefs described above may need to be restricted.

Nevertheless, it remains possible for the landlord and their family to use the property privately as a second home during the 'off season' and still fit within the qualifying conditions set out in Section 1.1. This opens up the possibility that, under the right circumstances, a furnished holiday letting property may also qualify for principal private residence relief and private letting relief (see the Taxcafe.co.uk guide *'How to Avoid Property Tax'* for further details).

However, whilst partial private use of the property carries some potential advantages, it is important to remember that the property must be let out on a commercial basis with a view to the realisation of profits. Hence, in practice, the property must be made available for letting to third parties for a sufficiently large proportion of the year to give its owners a realistic expectation of profits.

The result of failing to meet this test would be the loss of furnished holiday letting status and hence the consequent loss of all the additional reliefs which that status provides.

More commonly, a furnished holiday letting property may qualify for principal private residence relief and private letting relief as a result of its occupation as the landlord's main residence at some other time during their ownership.

1.3   DISADVANTAGES

The furnished holiday letting regime does carry some minor disadvantages, most notably:

- The 10% wear and tear allowance is not available.
- The landlords' energy-saving allowance is not available.
- It would not generally be possible for a furnished holiday letting property to qualify for rent-a-room relief.

In addition, the letting of holiday accommodation is a standard-rated supply for VAT purposes. This is a consequence of VAT legislation rather than the furnished holiday letting regime and is not dependent on whether the property meets the qualifying conditions set out in Section 1.1.

A landlord must therefore register for VAT if annual income from UK holiday lets exceeds £68,000. Foreign VAT registration will also often be required in respect of holiday lettings elsewhere within the European Union (see Appendix B).

As far as Stamp Duty Land Tax is concerned, furnished holiday lets are treated like any other residential property. The Stamp Duty Land Tax threshold for residential property was reduced back to its former level of £125,000 on 1st January 2010 and this will lead to extra costs of up to £1,750 on some transactions.

Properties used as holiday lets with the intention of letting the property for short periods totalling 140 days or more in the tax year are subject to Business Rates rather than Council Tax. Although the intended rental period is the same as under test (iv) in Section 1.1, this rule is not dependent on the furnished holiday letting regime.

1.4   SOME TERMINOLOGY

Properties which meet the conditions set out in Section 1.1 and thus qualify under the furnished holiday letting regime may variously be referred to as furnished holiday lettings, furnished holiday lets or qualifying furnished holiday accommodation. These terms all mean the same thing.

The UK tax year runs from 6th April in one calendar year to 5th April in the next calendar year. The current UK tax year is therefore the year ending 5th April 2010 and this is commonly referred to as 2009/10.

Individuals with any form of property rental business, including furnished holiday lets, should generally prepare accounts for the tax year. Companies may choose their own accounting periods.

1.5   SPOUSES AND PARTNERS

Throughout this guide, you will see me refer to 'married couples', spouses or husbands and wives.

It is important to remember that, unless specified to the contrary, the tax treatment being outlined applies to legally married couples only.

Civil Partnerships

Since December 2005, same sex couples have been able to enter into a civil partnership affording them all of the same legal rights and obligations as a married couple. This equality of treatment extends to all UK tax law.

Again, the couple will need to be in a legally registered civil partnership for this to apply. Otherwise, they will remain in the same position as any other unmarried couple.

Unlike many other countries, the UK has refused to adopt the term 'marriage' for a same sex couple entering a civil partnership. Nevertheless, any references to 'married couples' throughout this guide should be taken to also include registered civil partnerships.

Similarly, any reference to the taxpayer's 'spouse' will also include their civil partner where relevant.

Unmarried Partners

As we shall see later, there are sometimes advantages to being in an unmarried couple. When I use the term 'unmarried partner' in this guide this means a member of a couple who are not married to each other and not in a civil partnership together. It also refers to a life partner and not to a business partner.

Chapter 2

What Will Happen on 6th April 2010?

2.1   FACING UP TO CHANGE

The Government proposes to abolish the tax regime for furnished holiday lettings with effect from 6th April 2010 and has only just provided details on the exact mechanics of the transition arising when the regime ends.

As with many of this Government's previous 'knee-jerk' reactions, it would seem that a radical change to the tax system is to be forced upon us at short notice without any serious thought having been given to the consequences!

The sensible approach would have been to delay the change in order to allow for a period of consultation. However, with a General Election looming within a matter of months, this may not have been considered desirable by those who wish to ensure that this change takes place.

There is, of course, a strong chance that the forthcoming General Election will bring about a change of Government. This begs the question of whether a different Government might restore the furnished holiday letting regime.

Personally, I would not pin my hopes on this possibility: not because I doubt the likelihood of a change of Government but because whoever wins the General Election will need to raise taxes wherever they can. Whatever any new Government might ideally prefer, they are unlikely to reverse a tax-raising measure already put in place before the election. Not within the foreseeable future, at least.

Landlords with furnished holiday lettings must therefore face up to the fact that the furnished holiday letting regime is about to end and should plan their best course of action before the change takes place.

2.2   A WAY OUT?

There seems to be a general suggestion from the Government that all furnished holiday lettings will become 'normal' rental property from 6th April 2010.

However, it is worth reflecting on the fact that the furnished holiday letting regime was originally introduced to resolve arguments over whether businesses of this kind should, in fact, be treated as a trade under general principles. Hotels and guest houses are trades, many caravan parks are trades, why not furnished holiday accommodation? Traces of this old debate can be seen in the fact that some local tax offices still insist on collecting Class 2 National Insurance on furnished holiday letting income.

There is therefore a good chance that a small proportion of furnished holiday letting properties could be treated as trading properties under general principles, along similar lines to a hotel or guest house.

This has both advantages and disadvantages and is also likely to be strongly resisted by HM Revenue and Customs. Nevertheless, trading status could be hugely beneficial in some cases and we will therefore look at this idea in more detail in Chapter 8.

2.3   PARADISE LOST

I've seen it happen before. Someone (usually the European Court of Justice) says the UK tax rules create an unfair advantage, so the Government says "OK then, we'll take it off everyone". That's exactly what's happening to the furnished holiday lettings regime. This year, it's been extended to the European Economic Area; next year it's being taken away altogether.

Despite my comments in the previous section, the vast majority of furnished holiday letting properties (i.e. those which cannot qualify as trading properties under general principles), will become 'normal' rental properties from 6th April 2010.

These properties will then cease to qualify for any of the reliefs which are specifically provided under the furnished holiday letting regime, including:

Capital Gains Tax

- Entrepreneurs' relief
- Rollover relief on replacement of business assets
- Holdover relief for gifts
- Relief for 'loans to traders'

Income Tax

- Capital allowances
- Loss relief against other (i.e. non-rental) income
- Relief for losses carried back to previous years
- Eligibility as 'earnings' for pension contribution purposes

The position for two other important reliefs: Capital Gains Tax incorporation relief and Inheritance Tax business property relief, is less clear-cut, as these do not necessarily depend on the furnished holiday letting regime. We will look at the position on these reliefs later.

The fact that holiday accommodation is a standard-rated supply for VAT purposes is not dependent on the furnished holiday letting regime. VAT will therefore continue to apply to income from furnished holiday lettings after 5th April 2010.

Likewise, furnished holiday letting properties will continue to be treated the same as any other residential property for Stamp Duty Land Tax purposes.

The Business Rates rules are also unaffected by the abolition of the furnished holiday letting regime.

2.4　SILVER LININGS

There isn't much good news about the abolition of the furnished holiday letting regime, but I would highlight three 'silver linings' in this dark cloud.

Firstly and most importantly: flexibility. Without the need to meet the qualifying conditions set out in Section 1.1, landlords will be able to run their furnished holiday letting businesses in the way that suits them best. If someone offers to rent the property for the whole summer, you will be able to take them up without fear of losing out on any of the tax reliefs provided by the current furnished holiday letting regime.

Wealth Warning

If your furnished holiday letting business is registered for VAT, a change to residential lettings may result in a recovery of VAT: i.e. you may need to pay back some of the VAT which you have previously claimed.

Secondly, from 2010/11, you will be able to claim the 10% wear and tear allowance on any furnished holiday letting property. In some cases, this may be more beneficial than the capital allowances available under the current regime.

Thirdly, you will also be eligible to claim the landlord's energy saving allowance on any furnished holiday letting property. This allowance enables you to claim immediate tax relief for up to £1,500 of qualifying energy saving expenditure per property per year. Without this special relief, this expenditure would be regarded as a capital item and hence disallowed.

Landlords with furnished holiday letting properties will therefore generally benefit by delaying any expenditure which qualifies for the landlord's energy saving allowance until after 5th April 2010.

Further details on both the 10% wear and tear allowance and the landlord's energy saving allowance can be found in the Taxcafe.co.uk guide *'How to Avoid Property Tax'*.

Chapter 3

Capital Gains Tax

3.1 CURRENT CAPITAL GAINS TAX RELIEFS

Furnished holiday lettings are currently treated as a qualifying business for the purposes of a number of important Capital Gains Tax reliefs, including entrepreneurs' relief, rollover relief, holdover relief and incorporation relief.

These important reliefs currently enable most furnished holiday letting landlords to sell properties with a low rate of tax or to replace them, give them to another person, or transfer them into a company, free from Capital Gains Tax altogether.

From 6th April 2010, however, most furnished holiday lettings will be treated the same as any other investment property and most of these transactions will give rise to a Capital Gains Tax bill at either 10% or 18% (possibly more if the Capital Gains Tax rate is increased after the election).

In this chapter we will therefore look in detail at each of the main Capital Gains Tax reliefs currently available on furnished holiday lettings and consider how landlords can benefit from the current regime while it still lasts.

3.2 ENTREPRENEURS' RELIEF

Under the current regime, furnished holiday lettings are a qualifying business for the purposes of entrepreneurs' relief.

Entrepreneurs' relief reduces the effective rate of Capital Gains Tax on qualifying disposals from 18% to 10%. This is achieved by exempting four ninths of the capital gain arising.

Example

Anneka has just one investment property and it qualifies as a furnished holiday let. In December 2009, she sells the property and realises a capital gain of £90,000.

She qualifies for entrepreneurs' relief, so four ninths of her gain is exempt, leaving her with a taxable gain of just £50,000 (ignoring her annual exemption for the sake of illustration).

Her Capital Gains Tax bill at 18% is therefore £9,000, which is equivalent to an effective rate of 10% on her total gain of £90,000.

In other words, where entrepreneurs' relief is available, the taxpayer pays Capital Gains Tax at 18% on five ninths of the gain; equivalent to an overall effective rate of 10%.

This effective rate of 10% is actually a maximum, since many such gains will also benefit from the annual exemption.

For example, if her 2009/10 annual exemption of £10,100 is also available, Anneka's gain will be further reduced to just £39,900 (£50,000 - £10,100), giving her a Capital Gains Tax bill at 18% of just £7,182: just under 8% of her total gain of £90,000.

Business Sales versus Property Sales

To qualify for entrepreneurs' relief on the sale of a furnished holiday letting property, the owner must have operated the furnished holiday letting business for a period of at least a year prior to the disposal of the property or prior to the cessation of the furnished holiday letting business.

Unlike the former business asset taper relief, entrepreneurs' relief is not available every time a qualifying business asset is sold.

Firstly, entrepreneurs' relief is subject to a lifetime limit of £1m of qualifying gains per person.

Secondly, entrepreneurs' relief is only available under certain restricted circumstances, including a sale of:

i) Shares in a qualifying company,
ii) A qualifying partnership share,
iii) A qualifying business or part of a qualifying business,
iv) Assets used in a qualifying business when sold within three years after that business's cessation.

A 'part' of a qualifying business must be capable of being run as a going concern in its own right in order to qualify for these purposes.

Sales before 6th April 2010

In my view, most property which qualifies as furnished holiday accommodation must be a 'part' of a business capable of being run independently of any other part of the business. Hence, my interpretation of the entrepreneurs' relief legislation is that a capital gain on the sale of qualifying furnished holiday accommodation should currently generally qualify for entrepreneurs' relief as long as:

a)   The property is still being used as qualifying furnished holiday accommodation at the time of sale, or

b)   The property is sold within three years of ceasing to be used as qualifying furnished holiday accommodation.

Whether, in practice, HM Revenue and Customs will agree with this interpretation where the taxpayer has more than one qualifying furnished holiday letting property and sells just one of them at any time before 6th April 2010 remains to be seen.

Maximum Qualifying Gains

Subject to the points discussed above, a property investor should be able to realise total capital gains of up to £1m on qualifying furnished holiday accommodation at a maximum effective Capital Gains Tax rate of just 10%. A couple investing in property jointly should be able to benefit from this rate on total gains of up to £2m.

Note, however, that each individual must personally have owned the property as a furnished holiday let for at least a year prior to the disposal or cessation of the business in order to qualify for entrepreneurs' relief.

Under current Government proposals, it is now too late for couples to transfer furnished holiday letting property into joint ownership and enable the transferee partner to benefit from entrepreneurs' relief on their share of the capital gain arising on disposal.

(The only way a transferee partner might benefit from entrepreneurs' relief is if a new Government were to repeal the proposed abolition of the furnished holiday letting regime after the election. Whilst this might be a possibility, it would be a brave person who gambled on this.)

Property Disposals after 5th April 2010

Under current Government proposals, furnished holiday lettings will cease to be a qualifying business for entrepreneurs' relief purposes with effect from 6th April 2010.

This will be treated as a 'deemed cessation' of the qualifying business on 5th April 2010.

This has three important consequences:

i)   Anyone beginning a furnished holiday letting business after 6th April 2009 will be unable to qualify for entrepreneurs' relief.

ii)   A disposal of a furnished holiday letting **business** after 5th April 2010 will not be eligible for entrepreneurs' relief, but

iii)   Subject to point (i), a disposal of a furnished holiday letting **property** still in use in the business at the time of the deemed cessation on 5th April 2010 will continue to be eligible for entrepreneurs' relief until 5th April 2013.

Points (ii) and (iii) may seem a little contradictory, but it is important to distinguish the sale of a property as a separate asset from the sale of a business.

As things stand under current proposals, in order to qualify for entrepreneurs' relief on the sale of a furnished holiday letting property at any time between 6th April 2010 and 5th April 2013, it appears that it will be necessary to ensure that the actual business is not also sold.

The position here is a little odd and certainly very counter-intuitive. It may therefore be amended before the transitional rules for the abolition of the furnished holiday letting regime are finalised.

Nevertheless, at the time of writing it appears that, in order to qualify for entrepreneurs' relief on a sale taking place between 6th April 2010 and 5th April 2013, the person selling the property must not also sell any goodwill and should not provide any customer lists or pass on any existing bookings or the benefit of any advertising already undertaken.

Sales of Former Furnished Holiday Letting Properties

Landlords whose furnished holiday letting business actually did cease before 6th April 2010 will also continue to be eligible for entrepreneurs' relief on a sale of their former furnished holiday letting properties at any time within three years of the actual date of cessation of the furnished holiday letting business provided that they did own the business for at least a year prior to cessation.

The continued availability of entrepreneurs' relief on a former furnished holiday letting property for three years after the cessation, or deemed cessation, of the furnished holiday letting business is unaffected by any subsequent use of the property.

Hence, for example, a landlord who used a property as a furnished holiday let for several years but changed it to a residential let on 1st June 2009 would continue to be eligible for entrepreneurs' relief on a sale of that property until 31st May 2012.

Creating a Disposal

As we have seen, to benefit from a maximum effective Capital Gains Tax rate of 10% on a furnished holiday letting property, it will generally be necessary to dispose of the property by 5th April

2013 (or within three years of the actual cessation of the furnished holiday letting business if this occurred before 6th April 2010). This can be achieved by selling the property to an unconnected third party or by transferring it to a company, a trust or another individual (but not your spouse or civil partner).

Wealth Warning

Transfers of property to companies, trusts or other individuals may give rise to Stamp Duty Land Tax liabilities. See Section 9.2 for further details.

As we shall see in Sections 3.4 and 3.6, it will generally be possible to transfer a furnished holiday letting property to a company, a trust or another individual by 5th April 2010 free from Capital Gains Tax. However, many owners of furnished holiday letting property may take the view that it is better to pay Capital Gains Tax at an effective rate of just 10% rather than run the risk of greater liabilities arising later.

Example

John has a furnished holiday letting property which he bought for £50,000 in 1985 and which is now worth £230,000. He wishes to 'crystallise' his existing capital gain of £180,000 at a maximum effective Capital Gains Tax rate of just 10% rather than risk paying a higher rate of tax at a later date. John therefore transfers the property to his daughter Valerie on 1st April 2010. Although he would be entitled to hold over the capital gain arising, he does not do so, and pays Capital Gains Tax on his disposal as follows:

Deemed Sale Proceeds (Market Value)	*£230,000*
Less Cost	*(£50,000)*

	£180,000
Less Entrepreneurs' Relief (four ninths)	*(£80,000)*

	£100,000
Less Annual Exemption	*(£10,100)*

	£89,900
	======
Capital Gains Tax at 18%:	*£16,182*

22

A few years later, Valerie sells the property for £300,000. Her Capital Gains Tax bill is as follows:

Sale Proceeds (Actual)	£300,000
Less Deemed Cost (Market Value on Transfer)	(£230,000)

	£70,000
Less Annual Exemption	(£10,100)*

	£59,900
	======
Capital Gains Tax at 18%:	£10,782

The total Capital Gains Tax paid by John and Valerie is thus £26,964. Let's compare this with how much John would have paid if he had held on to the property himself until the time of the sale:

Sale Proceeds (Actual)	£300,000
Less Cost (Actual)	(£50,000)

	£250,000
Less Annual Exemption	(£10,100)*

	£239,900
	======
Capital Gains Tax at 18%:	£43,182

(We are assuming here that this hypothetical sale takes place after 5th April 2013, so that John is ineligible for entrepreneurs' relief.)

As we can see, the Capital Gains Tax paid by John on a sale of the property after 5th April 2013 without the benefit of entrepreneurs' relief is £16,218 (£43,182 - £26,964) more than the total tax payable if he had transferred the property to his daughter.

Valerie would also face the same tax bill on the ultimate sale if John held over his capital gain on the transfer (although in Section 3.4 we will see how to refine the position a little).

Furthermore, if the Capital Gains Tax rate were to increase before the ultimate sale, the additional tax arising would be even more. For example, with a Capital Gains Tax rate of, say, 25% on the ultimate sale, the transfer from John to Valerie would save £28,818.

* - For the sake of illustration, I have assumed no increase in the Capital Gains Tax annual exemption.

The example clearly demonstrates that there are considerable potential long-term savings to be made by transferring a furnished holiday letting property before 6th April 2010 without any hold over relief claim. The drawback, however, is that the Capital Gains Tax arising on the transfer will be payable by 31st January 2011, with no sale proceeds to fund it (often known as a 'dry tax charge').

Under current proposals, John could, in fact, achieve much the same result by transferring the property (but not the business) to Valerie at any time between 6th April 2010 and 5th April 2013 (holdover relief would not be available, but John is choosing not to claim it anyway).

This would, however, leave John exposed to the risk of an increase in the Capital Gains Tax rate before the transfer.

This is a difficult choice. Delaying the transfer will postpone the dry tax charge and could also increase the proportion of the overall gain which benefits from entrepreneurs' relief. On the other hand, it could increase the proportion of the gain which is subject to a future increase in the Capital Gains Tax rate.

3.3   ROLLOVER RELIEF

Where a qualifying asset is sold and the sale proceeds are reinvested in a new qualifying asset within the four year period beginning one year before, and ending three years after, the date of sale of the old asset, the taxpayer may claim to 'roll over' the capital gain arising on the sale of the old asset.

Example

Peter sold a furnished holiday letting property for £100,000 in July 2009 and reinvested the sale proceeds in a new furnished holiday letting property in March 2010. Peter realised a capital gain of £60,000 on the old property but claims roll over relief on his reinvestment rather than face any immediate Capital Gains Tax liability.

The new property cost £220,000 but, for Capital Gains Tax purposes, it will be treated as if it cost £160,000: i.e. £220,000 less the held over gain of £60,000.

At present, rollover relief is available in respect of both gains arising on disposals of qualifying furnished holiday accommodation and gains arising on disposals of trading property and other eligible assets which are reinvested in qualifying furnished holiday accommodation.

However, under current Government proposals, furnished holiday lettings will cease to qualify for rollover relief after 5th April 2010.

Nevertheless, taxpayers will still be able to avoid any immediate Capital Gains Tax liability under any of the following circumstances:

i) A sale of qualifying furnished holiday accommodation before 6th April 2010 which is reinvested in new furnished holiday letting property before 6th April 2010,

ii) A sale of qualifying furnished holiday accommodation before 6th April 2010 which is reinvested in trading property or other eligible assets at any time within the period beginning one year before the sale and ending three years after it,

iii) A sale of trading property or other eligible assets which is reinvested in new furnished holiday letting property purchased before 6th April 2010 and within the period beginning one year before the sale and ending three years after it.

Eligible gains may also be rolled over into capital improvements to qualifying furnished holiday accommodation carried out before 6th April 2010.

Note that newly acquired property into which a previous gain is rolled over only needs to be used as a furnished holiday let (or trading property) by the purchaser; it does not matter what the vendor was using it for.

'Trading property' in this context means a property used in your own trade, such as a hotel, a guest house, a shop, or trading premises for a property development or other trading business.

It is worth noting that many of the sales listed above would give rise to Capital Gains Tax at a maximum effective rate of just 10% and, as we saw in Section 3.2, it may often be better to pay this tax now rather than face greater liabilities in the future.

Action to Take by 5th April 2010

Anyone wishing to change their furnished holiday letting property portfolio should consider both selling the old properties and acquiring the new ones before 6th April 2010 in order to benefit from rollover relief.

Anyone wishing to invest the proceeds of sale of other trading property into qualifying furnished holiday accommodation should also consider doing so before 6th April 2010.

Action which can be Taken Later

There is a little less pressure for anyone wishing to reinvest the proceeds of sale of furnished holiday letting property into other trading property. In this case, it will only be necessary to sell the furnished holiday letting property before 6th April 2010: the gain arising can then be rolled over by reinvesting the sale proceeds in new trading property at any time within the usual three year time limit described above.

Existing Rolled Over Gains at 6th April 2010

Any existing gains rolled over into furnished holiday letting property which is still held on 6th April 2010 will only become taxable if and when that property is disposed of – i.e. on a future sale or lifetime transfer.

It will not usually be possible to roll over the gain again but entrepreneurs' relief should generally be available where the disposal takes place before 6th April 2013 or within three years of the cessation of the furnished holiday letting business if this occurred before 6th April 2010 (see Section 3.2).

There is also the opportunity to roll over eligible gains by acquiring a furnished holiday letting property before 6th April 2010 which can later be changed into a normal residential let, or even adopted as your own home. In the latter case, this might even enable you to avoid Capital Gains Tax on the rolled over gain altogether.

However, whilst furnished holiday letting properties will automatically cease to qualify for rollover relief on 6th April 2010, any rollover relief claim made on a purchase of such a property during 2009/10 will only be valid if the property does continue to be used as a furnished holiday let for a reasonable period thereafter (see Section 9.1 for details).

Preserving Rollover Relief

Any property still in use purely as a furnished holiday let on 6th April 2010 will cease to be eligible for roll over relief.

However, where all or part of the property is in some other qualifying use, the previous period of use as a furnished holiday let will continue to provide a proportionate eligibility for roll over relief.

Example

Maggie has a three storey property which she purchased on 1st March 1992. Since then, she has rented the property out as three luxury flats, all in use as qualifying furnished holiday accommodation.

27

On 1st March 2010, Maggie ceases her furnished holiday letting business and adopts the ground floor flat as her business premises for a new venture: a property development trade. She lets the other two flats out as residential property.

On 1st March 2012, Maggie sells the property and reinvests the proceeds in new business premises for her property development trade. She realises a capital gain of £2m on the old property.

The whole property was in qualifying business use for 18 years out of her total ownership period of 20 years and, for the last two years, one third of the property was in qualifying business use. Maggie can therefore claim to roll over the following part of her gain:

£2m x 18/20 =	*£1,800,000*
£2m x 2/20 x 1/3 =	*£66,667*
Total	*£1,866,667*

This leaves a gain of just £133,333. As Maggie sold the property within three years of ceasing her furnished holiday letting business, she is able to claim entrepreneurs' relief, giving her an effective Capital Gains Tax rate of just 10% and a Capital Gains Tax bill of just £13,333.

If Maggie had not adopted part of the property as her own trading premises, she would not have been eligible for any roll over relief and would have faced a Capital Gains Tax bill of at least £280,000 (£1m x 18% + £1m x 10% due to entrepreneurs' relief); possibly more if she had made any previous entrepreneurs' relief claims.

(The annual exemption has been ignored in this example for ease of illustration.)

3.4   HOLDOVER RELIEF

In principle, where a property is gifted, or sold at undervalue, to a 'connected person' (other than the transferor's spouse or civil partner), the transferor is treated as if they had sold the property for its current market value. We saw the effect of this in the 'John and Valerie' example in Section 3.2.

'Connected persons' for this purpose are listed in Appendix C. However, in practice, a gift or sale at undervalue to any other person is generally also treated as a sale at market value, as it is not a 'bargain at arms' length'.

At present, the capital gain arising on a gift, or transfer at undervalue, of a furnished holiday letting property can be 'held over'.

This requires a joint election by the transferor and transferee (except in the case of a transfer into trust when only the transferor needs to make the election).

In the case of a gift, the effect of such an election is that the transferor escapes Capital Gains Tax and the transferee is treated as if they had bought the property for its market value less the amount of the held over gain. Generally this works out the same as if the transferee had bought the property for the same price that the transferor originally bought it for.

Example

In March 2010, Lesley gives her son Jason a furnished holiday letting property. Lesley bought the property for £30,000 many years ago and it is currently worth £100,000. Lesley and Jason jointly elect to hold over the capital gain arising of £70,000.

Lesley has no Capital Gains Tax to pay on the transfer and Jason is treated as if he had bought the property for its current market value of £100,000 less the held over gain of £70,000. This equates to £30,000 – the same as Lesley's original purchase price.

In the case of a sale at undervalue, the effect of a holdover election is effectively to reinstate the actual sale price. This will reduce or eliminate the transferor's Capital Gains Tax bill but will mean that the transferee is subject to Capital Gains Tax on the ultimate sale of the property based on the excess of the ultimate sale price over the actual amount paid for the purchase.

A partial hold over of this nature can be used as a tax free mechanism for increasing the eligible base cost of the property in the transferee's hands, leading to a reduction in the Capital Gains Tax payable on an ultimate sale.

Example

Rather than gifting her furnished holiday letting property to Jason, Lesley decides instead to sell it to him for £48,180. Lesley and Jason now jointly elect to hold over the unrealised capital gain of £51,920 (£100,000 - £48,180), i.e. the excess of the property's market value over the actual sale price.

Lesley remains taxable on her 'realised' capital gain, as follows:

Deemed Sales Proceeds (Market Value)	*£100,000*
Less Cost	*(£30,000)*

	£70,000
Less Held Over Gain	*(£51,920)*

	£18,180
Less Entrepreneurs' Relief (four ninths)	*(£8,080)*

	£10,100
Less Annual Exemption	*(£10,100)*

Taxable Gain	*NIL*
	=======

As we can see, Lesley has no taxable gain and therefore still has no Capital Gains Tax to pay. At the same time, Jason is now treated as if he had bought the property for its market value of £100,000 less the held over gain of £51,920. This time, this works out at £48,180: the same as the transfer price.

The transfer is still tax free but Jason now has an eligible base cost of £48,180, or £18,180 more than in our previous example. This would save him £3,272 on a sale of the property at the current Capital Gains Tax rate of 18%; possibly more in the event of any future increase in the Capital Gains Tax rate.

This saving can generally be achieved by transferring property for a price equal to £18,180 more than the transferor's original purchase price. The transfer will still be tax free provided that the transferor is eligible for entrepreneurs' relief (see Section 3.2) and has not used their annual exemption elsewhere.

Practical Pointer

The transferee does not necessarily need to pay the purchase price in cash. If desired, the price can be set out in the purchase agreement but left outstanding as a loan.

Note, however, that such a loan remains part of the transferor's estate for Inheritance Tax purposes.

Wealth Warning

Where the actual purchase price exceeds £125,000 (or £175,000 before 1st January 2010) Stamp Duty Land Tax will be payable in the usual way.

Action to Take by 5th April 2010

Under current Government proposals, the facility to hold over the capital gain arising on a gift, or transfer at undervalue, of furnished holiday letting property to another individual will cease to apply after 5th April 2010.

Owners of furnished holiday letting property should therefore consider whether it might be appropriate to pass the property to another person before 6th April 2010 whilst this can still be done tax free. Typically, furnished holiday letting property owners might use this as an opportunity to pass wealth to an adult child.

The gift of property (or sale at undervalue) may be a potentially exempt transfer for Inheritance Tax purposes, or may even be exempt in some cases (see Chapter 7 for further details).

Holdover Relief after 5th April 2010

After the abolition of the furnished holiday letting regime, it will still be possible to hold over the capital gain arising on a lifetime transfer of a furnished holiday letting property into a trust.

However, whilst this mechanism will still exist, it has some major drawbacks compared with the hold over relief currently available. Most notably:

- A lifetime transfer into trust may give rise to Inheritance Tax charges.

- Where Capital Gains Tax holdover relief is claimed on a transfer of property into (or out of) trust, the property will subsequently be ineligible for principal private residence relief.

The second point means that the planning opportunity described in the next section will no longer be available after 5th April 2010.

3.5   TAX-FREE HOLIDAY HOMES

Until 5th April 2010, there is a fairly easy way to shelter the entire capital gain on a qualifying furnished holiday letting property.

If the property has never been used for any other purpose then the entire capital gain arising on a gift of the property can be held over where a joint election is made by the transferor and the transferee.

If the transferee then adopts the property as their main residence, any capital gain arising when they sell it, including the original held over gain, will be fully exempt.

Example

Petra has a flat in Edinburgh, which she has let out as furnished holiday accommodation for many years and has never used for any other purpose. The flat now stands at a substantial capital gain.

Petra can, however, gift the flat to her adult daughter, Freda, at any time up until 5th April 2010, and jointly elect with her to hold over the capital gain arising.

Freda can then make occasional (but regular) personal use of the property as a holiday home and can elect for it to be regarded as her main residence for Capital Gains Tax purposes.

Potentially, Freda's election in favour of the flat could be for as little as one week, thus preserving most of the Capital Gains Tax exempt status on her own home.

Freda will, however, need to adopt the flat as her holiday home for considerably longer – probably at least a year. In other words, it can be her main residence, by election, for just a week, but must actually be used as a second home for a much longer period.

The flat may then be sold at any time within three years of the date of Petra's gift and will be totally exempt from Capital Gains Tax.

It is probably advisable that Freda does not let out the flat for a reasonable period (say a year) and that period must include the period during which she has elected the property as her main residence.

Like any other gift or transfer, Petra should avoid any personal use of the flat after her gift to Freda. See Section 9.3 for further details.

3.6   INCORPORATION RELIEF

Where a qualifying business is transferred to a company wholly in exchange for shares in that company, the gain arising on the transfer may be held over into those shares. This is known as 'incorporation relief'.

Where the business is transferred partly in exchange for shares, then part of the gain is held over.

Example

Simon has a furnished holiday letting business with a total current value of £1,250,000. The original cost of the properties comprised in the business totals £250,000.

In January 2010, Simon transfers his business to a company in exchange for £22,725 in cash plus 200,000 ordinary shares.

Simon's total gain is £1,000,000 (£1,250,000 - £250,000) and this is allocated as follows:

Cash: £22,725 x £1,000,000/£1,250,000 = £18,180

Shares: £1,000,000 - £18,180 =   £981,820

The gain allocated to the cash is taxable immediately. However, after entrepreneurs' relief and his annual exemption, Simon will be left with no tax to pay.

The gain allocated to the shares is deducted from their market value of £1,227,275 (£1,250,000 - £22,725), meaning that Simon will be treated as if he had bought the shares for £245,455 (£1,227,275 - £981,820).

The Good News

Despite the fact that his properties stood at a gain of £1m, Simon is able to transfer them all to the company free from Capital Gains Tax.

The company is now treated as if it had bought the properties for their current values, totalling £1,250,000. It will only be taxed on any excess over these values when subsequently selling any of the properties.

The Bad News

As explained in Section 9.2, the company will pay Stamp Duty Land Tax on the total market value of the transferred properties. In this case, this amounts to £50,000 (£1,250,000 x 4%).

If Simon subsequently sells or winds up the company, he will be subject to Capital Gains Tax on the amount by which his net proceeds exceeds his eligible cost of £245,455.

On Balance

If you can cope with the initial Stamp Duty Land Tax cost of up to 4% of your portfolio's total current market value, incorporation relief provides a very useful mechanism for generating a tax-free uplift in the eligible cost of your properties.

Thereafter, instead of you paying Capital Gains Tax on the difference between your properties' original cost and sale proceeds, your company will only pay Corporation Tax on the difference between your properties' market values at the time of the transfer and their ultimate sale proceeds.

The company will also benefit from indexation relief on any future capital gains arising, although this needs to be weighed up against the higher Corporation Tax rate on capital gains when compared with the current low rate of Capital Gains Tax: 18%.

Whether incorporation relief will actually provide any long-term saving depends on your future investment strategy. If you intend to use the company for many years to come, and to make many changes to your property portfolio in that time, then incorporation relief is likely to save you a great deal in tax. If, however, you simply sell off your existing portfolio and wind the company up, you could be much worse off.

Example Part 2

A few years after transferring his portfolio to the company, Simon sells one of the properties. The property originally cost £50,000, was worth £250,000 at the time of the transfer, and sells for £300,000.

Inflation (based on the Retail Prices Index) has totalled 10% over the period since the transfer of the property. The company pays Corporation Tax on the gain arising as follows:

Sale Proceeds		£300,000
Less Deemed Cost:		
Market Value on Transfer	£250,000	
Stamp Duty Land Tax Paid on Transfer	£10,000	

		£260,000

		£40,000
Less Indexation Relief		
£260,000 x 10% =		£26,000

		£14,000
		=======
Corporation Tax payable at 22%:		£3,080

Note that the Stamp Duty Land Tax paid on the transfer was at 4% of the property's market value due to the 'linked transactions' rules (see Section 9.2).

The Corporation Tax rate applying is based on the assumptions that the small companies rate of Corporation Tax will be increased to 22% from 1ˢᵗ April 2011 (as currently proposed) and that the company's total profits and gains in the year of the sale do not exceed £300,000.

The total tax cost on this property amounts to £13,080 (£10,000 in Stamp Duty Land Tax plus £3,080 in Corporation Tax).

Let's compare this with the Capital Gains Tax cost which would have arisen if Simon had retained the property personally up until the time of the sale. Here, we will assume that the sale takes place after 5ᵗʰ April 2013, so that Simon is unable to claim entrepreneurs' relief (see Section 3.2).

Sale Proceeds	*£300,000*
Less Cost	*£50,000*

	£250,000
Less Annual Exemption	*£10,100*

	£239,900
	=======
Capital Gains Tax at 18%	*£43,182*

As we can see, by transferring his portfolio to the company, Simon has saved £30,102 (£43,182 - £13,080) on one property alone.

If the same pattern were repeated for his entire portfolio, Simon would save a total of £150,510, or over 10% of his total sales proceeds.

This is fine if Simon then simply reinvested his net proceeds within his company.

If, however, Simon were to then wind up his company, he would face an additional Capital Gains Tax charge.

Example Part 3

Simon has sold his entire property portfolio for a total of £1,500,000 over a few years.

Let us assume that the portfolio was made up of five properties, each of equal value to the one we looked at in Part 2 above. The total Corporation Tax arising on the sales will therefore have amounted to £15,400 (£3,080 x 5).

Let us also assume that the company borrowed £50,000 to pay the Stamp Duty Land Tax on the initial transfer of the properties. The net sales proceeds remaining in the company therefore total £1,434,600 (£1,500,000 - £15,400 - £50,000).

When Simon winds up the company, his Capital Gains Tax charge will be as follows:

Disposal Proceeds	*£1,434,600*
Less Deemed Cost	*£245,455*

	£1,189,145
Less Annual Exemption	*£10,100*

	£1,179,045
	=========
Capital Gains Tax at 18%	*£212,228*

Adding Simon's Capital Gains Tax to the Stamp Duty Land Tax and Corporation Tax paid by the company produces a total tax cost of £277,628 (£212,228 + £50,000 + £15,400).

Comparing this with the total Capital Gains Tax cost of £215,910 (£43,182 x 5) if Simon had retained the properties personally until sale, we can see that the incorporation has actually cost Simon an extra £61,718.

Furthermore, if Simon had kept the properties personally and sold them all by 5th April 2013, he would have been entitled to entrepreneurs' relief on the first £1m of his gains. This could have reduced his total Capital Gains Tax bill to just £137,728 if he had timed things right (sales in four different tax years = four annual exemptions).

He would not, however, be able to claim any entrepreneurs' relief on his company shares, even if he wound up the company by 5th April 2013. This is because the company would not have carried on a qualifying business for the required minimum one year period.

In this case, the incorporation would therefore have been quite disastrous, as it would have cost Simon total extra tax of £139,900 (£277,628 - £137,728).

Simon could reduce his total tax burden by disclaiming incorporation relief on the initial transfer of his properties into the company. This would give rise to an immediate Capital Gains Tax charge of £98,182 (£981,820 x 5/9 x 18%), but would reduce the Capital Gains Tax on the eventual winding up of the company to £35,501 (£1,434,600 - £1,227,275 - £10,100 = £197,225 x 18% = £35,501).

The total long-term tax cost without incorporation relief would thus be £199,083 (£98,182 + £50,000 + £15,400 + £35,501). This represents:

- A saving of £78,545 compared with the position where Simon did claim incorporation relief;

- A saving of £16,827 compared with the position where Simon retained the properties personally and sold them after 5th April 2013;

- But still costs £61,355 more than the position where Simon retained the properties personally and sold them all by 5th April 2013.

As we can see, an incorporation will not usually be desirable where you intend to sell your furnished holiday letting properties by 5th April 2013.

In other cases, a disclaimer of incorporation relief may seem like the ideal solution, producing the lowest long-term tax costs, but the problem is that the transfer of the portfolio to the company would then have 'up front' tax costs in both Capital Gains Tax and

Stamp Duty Land Tax, generally at 10% and either 3% or 4% respectively.

In Simon's case, for example, these 'up front' costs would amount to a total of £148,182 with no sales proceeds to pay them from.

Smaller Furnished Holiday Letting Businesses

Simon faces the problem of paying Stamp Duty Land Tax at 4% on the total market value of his furnished holiday letting portfolio.

A landlord with one or more furnished holiday letting properties worth no more than £125,000 in total could, however, transfer them to a company with no Stamp Duty Land Tax cost. By also claiming incorporation relief, such a transfer would be completely tax-free.

Furnished holiday letting property portfolios worth between £125,001 and £250,000 in total could be transferred for a Stamp Duty Land Tax cost of just 1% and those between £250,001 and £500,000 for 3%.

To reduce the Stamp Duty Land Tax cost, landlords with large furnished holiday letting businesses may wish to consider transferring only part of their portfolio to a company.

Transferring only part of your business may mean that incorporation relief is not available (as the whole of a business must be transferred to obtain the relief) but, as explained in Section 3.2, entrepreneurs' relief should usually be available to reduce the Capital Gains Tax arising on a transfer made before 6th April 2010 to a maximum effective rate of just 10%.

Furthermore, as we saw above, paying Capital Gains Tax on the initial transfer rather than claiming incorporation relief may actually prove more beneficial overall in the long run.

Earlier Incorporations

In our example, we saw that Simon was unable to claim entrepreneurs' relief on the winding up of his company, even if he did this by 5th April 2013, as the company had not carried on a qualifying business for the required minimum period of at least a year.

However, where a company carried on a furnished holiday letting business for a period of at least a year ending on or before 31st March 2010, the shares in that company may still qualify for entrepreneurs' relief on any disposal (e.g. a winding up, transfer, or sale) taking place before 1st April 2013 (or within three years of the cessation of the furnished holiday letting business if this occurred before 1st April 2010).

Various other qualifying conditions must also be met in order to obtain entrepreneurs' relief on a disposal of company shares. These are set out in the Taxcafe.co.uk guide *'Using a Property Company to Save Tax'*.

Action to Take by 5th April 2010

Furnished holiday letting businesses automatically qualify for incorporation relief until 5th April 2010.

Where incorporation relief is disclaimed, most transfers of furnished holiday letting properties to a company made before 6th April 2010 will qualify for entrepreneurs' relief.

Hence, whether incorporation relief is claimed or not, anyone considering transferring their furnished holiday letting business to a company should seriously consider doing so before 6th April 2010.

Transfers of Furnished Holiday Letting Properties to Companies after 5th April 2010

Most Capital Gains Tax reliefs generally only apply to trading businesses but are currently also available to qualifying furnished holiday accommodation under the special provisions of the furnished holiday letting regime.

Unusually, however, incorporation relief is available on the transfer of any 'business' to a company in exchange for shares.

Hence, whilst furnished holiday letting businesses will cease to automatically qualify for incorporation relief after 5th April 2010, many of the more substantial furnished holiday letting businesses might still qualify for the relief under general principles.

However, case law on the matter is far from clear and the transitional rules published on 9th December 2009 were silent on the subject. The position after 5th April 2010 will therefore be uncertain at best.

The position regarding entrepreneurs' relief on the transfer of furnished holiday letting properties to a company between 6th April 2010 and 5th April 2013 is also unclear. As discussed in Section 3.2, it currently appears that entrepreneurs' relief will only be available on disposals of furnished holiday letting properties as separate assets during this period and not on sales or transfers of furnished holiday letting businesses.

It is difficult to see how a transfer of furnished holiday letting properties to your own company could fail to be a transfer of a business unless you cease that business before the transfer. This, of course, then guarantees that you will not be eligible for incorporation relief.

So, in short, you can either:

a)   Transfer a continuing furnished holiday letting business in exchange for shares and hope that you will qualify for incorporation relief; or

b)   Cease the business and transfer the properties before 6th April 2013 (and within three years of cessation) so that you can claim entrepreneurs' relief.

Without either incorporation relief or entrepreneurs' relief, a transfer of a furnished holiday letting business to a company after 5th April 2010 will give rise to Capital Gains Tax at 18% and Stamp Duty Land Tax at up to 4% of the portfolio's total market value.

The best advice must therefore continue to be that, if incorporation of a furnished holiday letting business is considered desirable, it should be done by 5th April 2010.

Wealth Warning

Any personal use of property following a transfer to a company should generally be avoided. See Section 9.3 for further details.

3.7   LOANS TO TRADERS

Where a person makes a loan to another person for use in a qualifying business and that loan later becomes irrecoverable, the lender may claim a capital loss for the amount of their loss.

Similarly, where you guarantee a loan which has been used in a qualifying business, you may also claim a capital loss for any payments you have to make under that guarantee.

This relief is available in respect of loans to your own company but loans to your spouse or civil partner do not qualify.

Furnished holiday letting is currently a qualifying business for the purposes of this relief.

Loans (or guarantees) made before 6th April 2010 to individuals or partnerships carrying on a furnished holiday letting business, or before 1st April 2010 to companies carrying on a furnished holiday letting business, will continue to qualify for the relief regardless of when the loan becomes irrecoverable.

Any loans or guarantees made on or after these dates will not qualify for the relief.

Chapter 4

Capital Allowances

4.1   THE CURRENT POSITION

Landlords owning qualifying furnished holiday accommodation may currently claim capital allowances on fixtures, fittings, furniture and equipment within the properties, including the new 'annual investment allowance' introduced in April 2008 which provides immediate 100% relief for qualifying expenditure of up to £50,000 each tax year.

Landlords owning furnished holiday letting property jointly (but not as a partnership) may be able to claim 100% relief on up to £50,000 of qualifying expenditure **each**. That's up to £100,000 per year for a couple owning property jointly.

Integral Features

The introduction of 'integral features' in April 2008 means that capital allowances are currently available on a large part of the purchase price of any qualifying properties, including the cost of:

- Electrical lighting and power systems
- Cold water systems
- Space or water heating systems, air conditioning, ventilation and air purification systems and floors or ceilings comprised in such systems*
- Lifts, escalators and moving walkways*
- External solar shading

In a nutshell: All the wiring, lighting, plumbing, heating and air conditioning in any qualifying furnished holiday accommodation purchased between 6th April 2008 and 5th April 2010 qualifies for capital allowances, with immediate 100% relief for the first £50,000 spent on these items in each tax year.

(* - These items qualified for capital allowances before 6th April 2008 but the annual investment allowance was not available then.)

Other Qualifying Expenditure within Furnished Holiday Letting Properties

In addition to the new class of integral features, many other items within qualifying furnished holiday accommodation already qualified for capital allowances before April 2008 and continue to do so until 5th April 2010. These include:

- Furniture
- White Goods (e.g. fridges, cookers, dishwashers, etc)
- Electrical Equipment (e.g. televisions, radios, vacuum cleaners, kettles, etc)
- Furnishings (e.g. curtains, cushions, blinds, rugs, etc)
- Sinks, baths, showers and sanitary ware
- Computer, telecommunication and surveillance systems, including wiring and other links
- Fire and burglar alarm systems, sprinklers and other fire-fighting equipment
- Decorative assets provided for tenants' enjoyment (e.g. paintings, ornaments, etc)

Other Qualifying Expenditure outside Furnished Holiday Letting Properties

In addition to qualifying items within furnished holiday letting property, landlords may also claim capital allowances on other equipment used in their business, such as:

- Integral features and other qualifying items (as listed above) contained within the landlord's own business premises (except decorative assets)
- Computers
- Office furniture
- Gardening and cleaning equipment not stored within the furnished holiday letting properties
- Advertising hoardings, signs and displays
- Vans
- Cars (although these are not eligible for the annual investment allowance or first year allowances)

Qualifying Expenditure

Qualifying assets are eligible for the same rate of capital allowances whether they are purchased separately or as part of the purchase of the property.

It is the date of the expenditure itself which determines the rate of allowances available. Hence, for example, a landlord installing a new central heating system into a furnished holiday letting property during 2009/10 would be eligible to claim the annual investment allowance on the cost of that system, even if the property itself was purchased many years earlier.

On the other hand, a landlord buying a new property during 2009/10 can allocate a reasonable proportion of the purchase price to the integral features and other qualifying items within the property. Such an allocation generally needs to be done by a qualified surveyor. The qualifying proportion will depend on the features present within the property.

To qualify for capital allowances, the purchaser only needs to adopt the property as a furnished holiday let (see Section 9.1). It does not matter whether the property was previously being used as a furnished holiday let by the vendor.

4.2   EXPENDITURE IN EXCESS OF £50,000 AND CARS

As explained in Section 4.1, landlords with furnished holiday letting businesses are entitled to capital allowances on a wide range of expenditure both within their furnished holiday letting properties and outside them.

The annual investment allowance provides immediate 100% relief for the first £50,000 of total qualifying expenditure in each tax year.

If the landlord spends a total of more than £50,000 in the tax year, they can allocate the annual investment allowance to whichever part of their expenditure they wish (except cars, assets acquired from connected persons and a few other exceptions – see Section 4.8 for further details). This is very useful since, for expenditure in excess of the annual investment allowance, different rates of capital allowances apply.

1. Integral Features and Cars with CO2 Emissions over 160g/km

These assets are added to the 'special rate pool'. The landlord may claim a writing down allowance equal to 10% of the balance of expenditure within the special rate pool each year.

The remaining 90% of the qualifying expenditure in the pool is carried forward to the next year.

2. Other Assets Within Furnished Holiday Letting Properties and Cars with CO2 Emissions no more than 160g/km

These assets are added to the 'general pool'. The landlord may claim a writing down allowance equal to 20% of the balance of expenditure within the general pool each year. The remaining 80% of the qualifying expenditure in the pool is carried forward to the next year.

There is a school of thought that qualifying assets within furnished holiday letting properties which are purchased during 2009/10, or before 6th April 2008, should be eligible for the first year allowance described below. Sadly, however, HM Revenue and Customs takes the view that first year allowances are not available on this expenditure. For a full analysis of the position on this type of expenditure see the Taxcafe.co.uk guide 'How to Avoid Property Tax'. Remember, however, that this is now only relevant where the landlord has total qualifying expenditure in the year in excess of £50,000.

3. Other Qualifying Expenditure

Any other qualifying expenditure is treated the same as under (2) above except where it is incurred during 2009/10 or was incurred before 6th April 2008.

For other qualifying expenditure incurred during 2009/10, a first year allowance of 40% is available instead of (not in addition to) the usual writing down allowance of 20%. The remaining 60% of the qualifying expenditure is added to the balance carried forward on the general pool.

Notes

i)   Different rates of allowances applied before 6th April
         2008.

ii)   Where the landlord also uses any asset privately, the
         capital allowances on the asset are restricted and it is
         kept separate from either of the 'pools'. This applies
         most commonly to cars but can also apply to other
         assets with private use. See Section 4.3 for further
         details.

iii)   Where the balance on either the general pool or the
         special rate pool falls below £1,000, the whole balance
         may be written off (i.e. claimed as an allowance) in the
         following year (provided that new additions in excess
         of the annual investment allowance do not take the
         balance back over £1,000 again).

Until the Pre-Budget Report on 9th December 2009, we did not
know what would happen to the remaining balance of
expenditure carried forward in the pools at 6th April 2010.

However, in the Pre-Budget Report, it was confirmed that capital
allowances will continue to be available on the balances carried
forward at that date. This is fantastic news for furnished holiday
letting landlords incurring qualifying expenditure before 6th April
2010 and we will look at the practical implications of this in
Sections 4.10 and 4.11.

Allocating the Annual Investment Allowance

Subject to any restrictions for private use applying (see Section
4.3), furnished holiday letting landlords who incur more than
£50,000 of qualifying expenditure can maximise their overall
capital allowances claim by allocating the annual investment
allowance first to expenditure under (1) above, then to
expenditure under (2) and then any remaining balance to
expenditure under (3).

Remember, however, that the annual investment allowance
cannot be claimed on cars or certain other purchases (see Section
4.8).

4.3   ASSETS WITH PRIVATE USE

Any asset which the landlord also uses privately is not added to either the general pool or the special rate pool.

Instead it is de-pooled and put in its own private use 'puddle'.

The same basic rate of allowances applies to assets in private use puddles as would have applied if there had been no private use, except that the allowance actually claimed must be restricted.

The restriction on the claim in respect of private use does not affect the balance of expenditure carried forward in the private use puddle.

Example

Angela buys a car for £20,000 and uses it 75% privately and 25% in her furnished holiday letting business. The car has CO2 emissions of 170g/km.

A writing down allowance of 10% is available on the car, i.e. £2,000. Angela will need to restrict her claim to just 25% of this amount, i.e. £500.

The balance of expenditure carried forward is £18,000 (£20,000 - £2,000). Next year, the writing down allowance available to Angela will be £1,800 (£18,000 x 10%) but she will again need to restrict her claim to just 25%, i.e. £450.

4.4   TAX RELIEF FOR CAPITAL ALLOWANCES

Capital allowances claimed by a furnished holiday letting landlord should be set against their furnished holiday letting profits in the first instance.

Any excess is then set against the landlord's other UK property income, or their other foreign property income in the case of qualifying furnished holiday accommodation elsewhere in the European Economic Area (but see Section 10.5 for some important further details on this).

If there is still an excess, this can <u>currently</u> be treated either as:

i)   A furnished holiday letting loss which can be set against the landlord's other income of the same tax year and the previous one. Losses arising during 2008/9 and 2009/10 may also be carried back and set off against profits from qualifying furnished holiday lets in the previous three years. See Section 5.1 for further details.

Or

ii) Excess capital allowances which can be set against the landlord's other income for the same tax year or the next one.

In essence, therefore, as long as the furnished holiday letting landlord has sufficient total income in the same year, the previous year, or the next year, they should always get tax relief for their capital allowances.

Even after the abolition of the furnished holiday letting regime on 6th April 2010, any future capital allowances in excess of the landlord's total UK property income (or foreign property income, as the case may be) will still be available to set off against their other income for the same tax year or the next one, as under point (ii) above.

This makes capital allowances for furnished holiday letting businesses a very powerful tax relief indeed.

Where the allowances still cannot be relieved in any of the ways described above, they can be carried forward as part of the landlord's rental losses to be set off against future rental income from UK property or foreign property, as the case may be (but see Section 10.5 regarding losses on foreign furnished holiday lets).

Capital allowances are not compulsory. The landlord may choose not to claim them or may claim any proportion of the available allowances.

Claiming less than your maximum entitlement is known as a capital allowances 'disclaimer'. A disclaimer may be beneficial when your total income would be less than your personal allowance if you were to claim your full entitlement.

Allowances disclaimed are not wasted – they are added to the balance carried forward on your general pool, special rate pool or personal use puddle, thus increasing your future allowances.

4.5 CAPITAL ALLOWANCES IN PRACTICE

We've now covered most of the theory behind the current capital allowances regime for furnished holiday letting businesses.

Before we move on to look at the impact of the abolition of the furnished holiday letting regime on capital allowances, it is worth us looking at a detailed example to illustrate the massive benefits currently available to furnished holiday letting landlords.

Example

On 6th April 2007, Duncan bought his first furnished holiday letting property in Devon. The capital allowances regime was less beneficial at that time (see Section 4.1), but Duncan was nevertheless still able to claim capital allowances on £20,000 worth of expenditure, including the property's heating system and all the furniture and equipment which Duncan purchased for it.

In 2007/8, Duncan claimed writing down allowances of £5,000 (under the old system then applying and following HM Revenue and Customs' view that first year allowances are not available), leaving a £15,000 balance of expenditure carried forward. This balance was carried forward in Duncan's general pool (the special rate pool only applies to expenditure incurred after 5th April 2008).

In 2008/9, Duncan was able to claim writing down allowances of 20% on the balance brought forward on his general pool. (Although the special rate pool would now apply to new expenditure, any existing balance in a general pool at 6th April 2008 remains there.)

This gave Duncan a capital allowances claim of £3,000 in 2008/9 and a balance of £12,000 carried forward on his general pool.

In February 2010, Duncan decides to expand his furnished holiday letting business and he buys several more properties throughout the West

Country. He also decides to fit out his spare bedroom at home as an office and he buys a computer and some office furniture. Lastly, he buys a car which he starts to use 60% in his furnished holiday letting business and 40% privately. The car has CO2 emissions of 150g/km.

Duncan's total qualifying expenditure for capital allowances purposes in 2009/10 is as follows:

Integral features within new properties	*£30,000*
Other qualifying assets within new properties	*£18,000*
Computer and office furniture	*£7,000*
Car	*£10,000*

Duncan allocates his £50,000 annual investment allowance to the integral features, the other qualifying assets within his new properties and £2,000 of his office furniture.

He then claims a first year allowance of 40% on the remaining £5,000 of expenditure on his computer and office furniture.

Finally, he can also claim a 20% writing down allowance on his car, although he will need to restrict this due to his partial private use of the car.

Duncan's total capital allowances claim for 2009/10 is as follows:

Annual investment allowance	*£50,000*
First year allowances (£5,000 x 40%)	*£2,000*
Writing down allowance on general pool	
(£12,000 brought forward x 20%)	*£2,400*
Writing down allowance on car	
(£10,000 x 20% x 60%)	*£1,200*
Total	*£55,600*

Duncan's rental profits for 2009/10, before capital allowances, are £30,000. He also has a salary of £70,000.

The first £30,000 of his capital allowances are automatically set off against his rental profits, saving him £12,000 in Income Tax.

The remaining £25,600 of Duncan's capital allowances can be set off against his salary. This will produce a tax repayment of £10,240 (£25,600 x 40%).

In total, Duncan's capital allowances claim saves him £22,240!

What Next for Duncan?

Duncan will have a balance of £12,600 (£12,000 - £2,400 + £5,000 - £2,000) to carry forward on his general pool and £8,000 (£10,000 - £2,000) on his car.

In Section 4.11 we will return to Duncan and see how he fares after the abolition of the furnished holiday letting regime on 6th April 2010.

4.6 NEW FURNISHED HOLIDAY LETTING BUSINESSES

In Duncan's case (see Section 4.5), it did not matter when during 2009/10 he bought the qualifying assets: he was still entitled to the full amount of capital allowances due for the year.

This is because Duncan already had an existing furnished holiday letting business before 6th April 2009, so his business existed for the whole of the 2009/10 tax year.

Where, however, a landlord starts a new furnished holiday letting business during the tax year, they will only be entitled to restricted allowances based on the length of time that they have the business during the year. This is generally based on the date of their first letting.

Both the annual investment allowance and the rate of writing down allowances would then be restricted, although the first year allowance remains the same, where available.

Example

Sarah had no furnished holiday letting business prior to 1st October 2009. On that date, however, she incurred exactly the same qualifying expenditure as Duncan in our previous example (see Section 4.5) and commenced a furnished holiday letting business.

There are 187 days in the period from 1ˢᵗ October 2009 to 5ᵗʰ April 2010 so Sarah's annual investment allowance will be restricted to £50,000 x 187/365 = £25,616.

She allocates this to the integral features in her properties, leaving her able to claim capital allowances for 2009/10 as follows:

Annual investment allowance	*£25,616*
Writing down allowance on integral features	
(£30,000 - £25,616 = £4,384 x 10% x 187/365)	*£225*
Writing down allowance on general pool*	
(£18,000 x 20% x 187/365)	*£1,844*
First year allowances on other qualifying assets	
(£7,000 x 40%)	*£2,800*
Writing down allowance on car	
(£10,000 x 20% x 187/365 x 60%)	*£615*
Total	*£31,100*

* - Based on the HM Revenue and Customs view that first year allowances are not available on any assets within furnished holiday letting properties. Note that there is no balance brought forward on the general pool as Sarah has only just commenced her furnished holiday letting business.

It can readily be seen that the capital allowances regime is far less beneficial for a new landlord who does not already have an existing furnished holiday letting business.

Nevertheless, Sarah's capital allowances claim could still save her up to £12,440 in Income Tax in 2009/10.

4.7   SALES, CESSATIONS AND GIFTS

When any asset on which capital allowances have been claimed is sold, an amount must be deducted from the general pool, special rate pool, or private use puddle (as applicable).

The amount to be deducted is the lower of:

a) The sales proceeds, or
b) The amount on which capital allowances were claimed (usually the original cost).

This includes integral features and other fixtures within a furnished holiday letting property at the time of sale (where capital allowances have been claimed on these items). A proportion of the sale price must therefore be allocated to these items. Normally, a reasonable allocation of the sale price must be made for this purpose.

It is, however, possible for the vendor and purchaser to jointly elect to use an agreed value (less than original cost) for the relevant assets within the property. This election, known as a 'Section 198 Election', is useful for vendors as it will reduce or eliminate any balancing charge (see below). The election tends to be less beneficial for the purchaser, however, as it restricts the allowances which they can claim: they must use the same value as their purchase cost for capital allowances purposes.

Fortunately for many purchasers at the moment, the Section 198 Election only covers features and fixtures within the property on which the vendor claimed capital allowances. In many cases, this will exclude most of the integral features, as the vendor cannot have claimed allowances on some of these if they purchased the property, or installed the features, before 6th April 2008.

Provided that the property is being sold for full market value, the Section 198 Election can still be used to eliminate any balancing charges for the vendor when the purchaser does not intend to adopt the property as a furnished holiday let themselves. In this case, there is no disadvantage for the purchaser, so the election will always be a good idea.

The same will apply to all sales of furnished holiday letting properties after 5th April 2010. The purchaser will be unable to claim any capital allowances on assets within the property, so a Section 198 Election can be used to eliminate any balancing charges for the vendor and the purchaser will not be losing out on anything.

Balancing Allowances and Charges

If the deduction arising on the sale leaves a positive balance, capital allowances continue as normal on the general pool or special rate pool. Any positive balance in a private use puddle is allowed as a balancing allowance (i.e. an extra capital allowance), subject to the usual restriction for private use.

If the deduction arising on the sale leaves a negative balance on any pool or puddle, this amount becomes a balancing charge: an extra taxable profit for the business. Balancing charges on private use puddles are restricted by the same proportion as the capital allowances previously given on the same asset.

Cessations

If a landlord ceases to use a property as a furnished holiday let before 6th April 2010, but without selling it, they are treated as if they had sold all of the assets within the property on which they had previously claimed capital allowances. The assets are treated as having been sold for their market value at the time that the property ceased to be used as a furnished holiday let.

The amount deducted from the general pool, special rate pool or private use puddle in respect of each relevant asset is therefore the lower of:

a) Its market value at the date of cessation, or
b) The amount on which capital allowances were claimed (again, usually the original cost).

As usual, this includes any features and fixtures on which the landlord had previously claimed any capital allowances. However, it would exclude any furniture or equipment which the landlord moved to another of their furnished holiday letting properties.

If a landlord ceases their furnished holiday letting business altogether before 6th April 2010, they are treated as if they had sold all the assets on which they had previously claimed any capital allowances for their market value at that date.

In the case of a complete cessation before 6th April 2010, a balancing allowance is given for any positive balances remaining in the general pool or special rate pool after deduction of the deemed sales proceeds (or original costs, if less).

For these purposes, any furnished holiday letting properties which a landlord has in other countries within the European Economic Area are treated as a separate business to any furnished holiday letting properties which they have in the UK.

Gifts and Sales at Below Market Value

For capital allowances purposes, a gift of a furnished holiday letting property is treated the same as if the property had been sold at market value **but** without the option of using a Section 198 election.

A gift of a furnished holiday letting property may therefore result in balancing charges.

A sale at below market value is generally subject to the same treatment except in the case of a sale before 6th April 2010 when the purchaser also adopts the property as a furnished holiday let. In this case, actual sales proceeds are used for capital allowances purposes. Alternatively, a Section 198 Election can be used to reduce any balancing charges.

> ### Tax Tip
>
> When transferring a furnished holiday letting property to another person (including a company or trust) before 6th April 2010, balancing charges can be avoided by making a sale at below market value (even for £1), rather than a gift, provided that the purchaser also uses the property as a furnished holiday let.

4.8   FRIENDLY PURCHASES

Sadly, neither the annual investment allowance nor any first year allowance is available in the case of assets acquired from a 'connected' person (see Appendix C). Hence, it will not be possible to obtain these allowances on assets within a furnished holiday letting property simply by selling it to a spouse, civil partner or adult child, or transferring it to a trust or company.

Such sales or transfers made before 6th April 2010 may still generate writing down allowances, however, and could therefore still be worthwhile in some cases. The position here is similar to an existing property which is 'adopted' as a furnished holiday let (see Section 4.9 below).

There is also a further anti-avoidance rule which denies any annual investment allowance where expenditure is incurred wholly or mainly for the purposes of obtaining the allowance and the expenditure is connected with a change in another person's business.

Conceivably, however, and subject to this anti-avoidance rule, a property could be purchased before 6th April 2010 from a person not deemed to be 'connected' (see Appendix C), such as an unmarried partner (i.e. a 'life partner', not a business partner), and adopted as a furnished holiday let (see Section 9.1) in order to provide up to £50,000 of immediate relief on the 'integral features' and other eligible assets within the property.

The anti-avoidance rule can only apply where the property is already a business property, so this would work where the property was the transferor's own home, for example.

In other cases, the purchase would need to be made for bona fide commercial reasons in order to get around the anti-avoidance rule. A good example would be an 80-year old man selling his furnished holiday letting business to his 55-year old unmarried life partner on the basis that he wishes to retire.

Such a sale might also yield balancing allowances for the vendor where the market value of furniture and equipment within the properties is less than the remaining balance on their general pool.

Remember, however, as explained in Section 4.6 above, that the purchaser's capital allowances will be restricted if they do not already have an existing furnished holiday letting business of their own.

4.9 ADOPTING AN EXISTING PROPERTY AS A FURNISHED HOLIDAY LET

In principle, capital allowances are available when a property owner adopts an existing property as a furnished holiday let (see Section 9.1 regarding how a property can be 'adopted' as a furnished holiday let). This applies equally to a property owner adopting their own home as a furnished holiday let or a landlord changing a normal residential letting into a furnished holiday let.

The same assets are eligible for capital allowances as in the case of a new property purchase (see Section 4.1). However, neither the annual investment allowance nor first year allowances may be claimed in respect of assets within the 'adopted' property.

All that would be available is writing down allowances at 10% on integral features and at 20% on other qualifying assets, based on the market value of those assets at the date that the property is 'adopted' as a furnished holiday let.

The allowances would be further restricted if the landlord did not already have an existing furnished holiday letting business (see Section 4.6).

However, as we shall see in Section 4.10, the remaining balances on the general and special rate pools would continue to attract capital allowances after 5th April 2010.

Adopting an existing property as a furnished holiday let before 6th April 2010 could therefore yield considerable future tax savings.

4.10 WHAT WILL HAPPEN ON 6TH APRIL 2010?

One of the most important questions about the abolition of the furnished holiday letting regime is: "What happens to capital allowances claimed up to 5th April 2010 when the furnished holiday letting regime is abolished?"

Thankfully, when we finally got an answer to this question on 9th December 2009, it was just about as good as we could possibly have hoped.

The new rules can be summarised as follows:

- Balances on the general pool, the special rate pool and any private use 'puddles' at 5th April 2010 will simply be carried forward as normal. There will not be any special balancing adjustments as a consequence of the abolition of the furnished holiday letting regime.

- If the landlord also has a 'normal' UK property business (or a 'normal' foreign property business, as the case may be), the carried forward balances in the general pool and special rate pool for the furnished holiday letting business will be combined with the balances on the general pool and special rate pool (respectively) for that 'normal' business.

- Writing down allowances will continue to be given on the carried forward balances in the usual way.

- Future purchases of furnished holiday letting properties, or of assets for use within furnished holiday letting properties, on or after 6th April 2010 will not be eligible for any capital allowances.

- Capital allowances will, however, continue to be available on new purchases of qualifying equipment and other assets used by the landlord which are not located within the furnished holiday letting properties. These were listed in Section 4.1 and might include the landlord's own computer, office furniture and car, for example.

- Capital allowances will also continue to be available on new purchases of qualifying assets which are not contained within individual dwellings. For example, a landlord purchasing an apartment block will be eligible for capital allowances on qualifying items not contained within any of the individual apartments. This would include the lifts and a proportion of any other integral features within the property.

- From 6th April 2010, the 10% wear and tear allowance will be available in respect of all furnished holiday letting properties, including those purchased before 6th April 2010 and regardless of the amount of capital allowances claimed on such properties. (For further details on the wear and tear allowance, see the Taxcafe.co.uk guide *'How to Avoid Property Tax'*.)

- Future sales of furnished holiday letting properties purchased before 6th April 2010 will continue to be treated as described in Section 4.7. Landlords will be able to use Section 198 Elections to eliminate most chargeable gains, although any sales proceeds received for individual items of furniture, etc, on which capital allowances have previously been claimed will need to be deducted from the general pool in the usual way.

- Both gifts and sales at below market value taking place on or after 6th April 2010 will generally be treated as sales at market value for capital allowances purposes. Section 198 Elections will not be available in these cases meaning that balancing charges may arise where the property was purchased before 6th April 2010.

- From 6th April 2010, a property will only be treated as ceasing to be used in the business if it ceases to be rented out altogether. Simply ceasing to use it as a furnished holiday let will no longer be relevant for capital allowances purposes.

- Similarly, the business itself will only be treated as ceasing if the landlord ceases to rent out any UK property (or foreign property, as the case may be).

Tax Tip

As explained in Section 4.7, it will often be possible to avoid any balancing charges on a sale of a furnished holiday letting property by using a Section 198 Election. This is particularly important for anyone claiming the annual investment allowance on integral features and other fixtures within a property purchased during 2008/9 or 2009/10.

It is not, however, possible to avoid balancing charges, based on the market value of qualifying assets on which capital allowances have been claimed, in the event that a property ceases to be used as a furnished holiday let before

6th April 2010, or ceases to be used as a rental property thereafter.

Similarly, balancing charges cannot be avoided in the case of a gift (at any time), or sale at below market value after 5th April 2010.

To avoid balancing charges on furnished holiday letting properties purchased before 6th April 2010, landlords should therefore either sell them for full market value (at any time), or sell them before 6th April 2010 to someone who will also adopt them as a furnished holiday let, and should **not**:

a) Adopt them as 'normal' rental properties before 6th April 2010,
b) Cease to use them as rental properties altogether at any time,
c) Gift them at any time, or
d) Sell them at below market value after 5th April 2010.

In essence, UK furnished holiday letting properties will, in future, be treated as part of a 'normal' UK property business and foreign furnished holiday letting properties within the European Economic Area will be treated as part of a 'normal' foreign property business. New additions on or after 6th April 2010 will be subject to the very restricted capital allowances rules applying to 'normal' property businesses but the allowances on existing assets already held at 5th April 2010 will continue as usual.

Landlords who also have commercial rental properties (shops, offices, etc) will continue to be eligible for capital allowances on qualifying expenditure within those properties after 5th April 2010.

In the next section, we will return to an earlier example to see the impact of the new capital allowances rules in practice.

In general, however, it is now clear that landlords will benefit by purchasing new furnished holiday letting properties and other eligible assets before 6th April 2010 in order to maximise their capital allowances claims in 2009/10 and in future years also.

4.11 THE NEW RULES IN PRACTICE

To see the impact of the new rules set out in Section 4.10 in practice, we will return to our friend Duncan (from Section 4.5) and see what happens to him.

Example Revisited

At 6th April 2010, Duncan had a brought forward balance of £12,600 on his general pool and £8,000 on his car.

As long as Duncan continues to have a UK property business, the capital allowances on his car should continue as normal. For the sake of illustration we will therefore ignore his car for the rest of this section.

It is also worth noting that Duncan would continue to be eligible for the annual investment allowance on new purchases of qualifying assets, other than cars, which are not located within his rental dwellings (see Section 4.1 for further details).

The really great, and slightly unexpected news, however, is that Duncan will also continue to be eligible for writing down allowances on the full balance of £12,600 brought forward on his general pool, even though some of this expenditure would no longer qualify for capital allowances if it had been incurred after 5th April 2010.

Hence, Duncan will be able to claim writing down allowances as follows:

2010/11:   £2,520 (£12,600 x 20%)
2011/12:   £2,016 (£12,600 - £2,520 = £10,080 x 20%)
2012/13:   £1,613 (£10,080 - £2,016 = £8,064 x 20%)
And so on.

Subject to any future disposals of assets on which he has claimed capital allowances (see Section 4.7), Duncan's capital allowances claim would continue in this way until he either ceased renting out one or more of his properties or the balance remaining on his general pool fell below £1,000 (see Note (iii) in Section 4.2).

As explained in Section 4.10, it would not matter if Duncan changed any of his furnished holiday letting properties to a normal residential let, as these are all treated as part of the same business from 6th April 2010.

As we can see, purchasing furnished holiday letting properties, or assets for use within those properties, before 6th April 2010 will not only provide substantial tax relief during 2009/10, but may also provide a continuing benefit thereafter.

Remember that future capital allowances can be set off against the landlord's other income (see Section 4.4), so that tax relief will be obtained even when the properties are not producing rental profits in future.

As noted in Section 4.10, it should be possible to avoid any balancing charges on a sale of furnished holiday letting properties after 5th April 2010 by using a Section 198 Election.

Properties can also be changed from furnished holiday lets to normal residential lets without affecting the landlord's capital allowances claim.

The only real area of difficulty comes in the case of furnished holiday letting properties purchased before 6th April 2010 which either cease to be rented out altogether at some point in the future or which are transferred or sold for less than full market value (meaning that no Section 198 Election is possible).

As explained in Section 4.7, all of the assets within the property on which capital allowances have been claimed must then be treated as if they had been sold for their market value at that date, thus potentially giving rise to substantial balancing charges – particularly for those landlords claiming the annual investment allowance in 2008/9 or 2009/10.

Example Continued

On 1st May 2013, Duncan gives one of the properties which he purchased in February 2010 to his daughter Yvette.

Duncan originally claimed capital allowances on £10,000 of integral features in the property and £6,000 worth of furniture and equipment.

By May 2013, the market value of the integral features is £12,000 and the market value of the furniture and equipment is £2,500. In each case, the lower of the original amount claimed and the current market value is the amount which must be deducted from Duncan's general pool, or special rate pool.

Hence, the sum of £2,500 is deducted from Duncan's brought forward general pool balance of £6,451 (£8,064 - £1,613), leaving a balance of just £3,951. This attracts a writing down allowance for 2013/14 in the usual way, i.e. £790 (£3,951 x 20%).

The sum of £10,000 is deducted from Duncan's special rate pool. Due to the annual investment allowance which he claimed in 2009/10, Duncan has a special rate pool with a balance of nil. The deduction therefore results in a balancing charge of £10,000.

Note that, in practice, the amounts to be deducted from the general and special rate pools should be calculated on an item by item basis, with the lower of current market value and the amount originally claimed for capital allowances taken as the deduction in each case.

Duncan originally claimed capital allowances of £55,600 in 2009/10 (see Section 4.5) and ends up suffering a net balancing charge of £9,210 (£10,000 - £790) in 2013/14.

For most higher rate taxpayers in a similar situation this would mean that they benefitted from a saving of £22,240 (£55,600 x 40%) in 2009/10 but suffered an extra tax cost of £3,684 (£9,210 x 40%) in 2013/14. This could also be termed as an absolute saving of £18,556 (£22,240 - £3,684) and a four year cashflow saving of £3,684: not a bad result!

The only people who might lose out are those with a higher marginal tax rate at the time of the property's disposal than they had at the time of the original capital allowances claim.

In practice, this might be difficult to foresee but, if the landlord can predict such an outcome, the best option would be to disclaim part of the capital allowances claim in 2008/9 or 2009/10 in order to preserve sufficient balance carried forward on either the general pool or special rate pool (as appropriate) to prevent the later balancing charge from arising.

Landlords have a little time to decide, as the capital allowances claim for 2008/9 can be amended up until 31st January 2011 and the claim for 2009/10 can be amended up until 31st January 2012.

Subject to this, it is clear that the vast majority of furnished holiday letting landlords will benefit by claiming the maximum possible capital allowances in 2009/10.

Even those who commence a new furnished holiday letting business during 2009/10 may benefit substantially in the long run.

Whilst their capital allowances claim for 2009/10 will be restricted and may be quite small in some cases, they will continue to be eligible for writing down allowances on the balances carried forward on their general and special rate pools for as long as they continue to have a property rental business.

And don't forget that all furnished holiday letting landlords will also be able to claim the 10% wear and tear allowance from 2010/11 onwards and this is completely unaffected by the amount of capital allowances claimed.

4.12   MAXIMISING CAPITAL ALLOWANCES

In this chapter we have seen that it will nearly always be beneficial for furnished holiday letting landlords to maximise their capital allowances claims in 2009/10. This can be achieved by doing one or more of the following before 6th April 2010:

- Purchasing furnished holiday letting property.
- Replacing or installing new 'integral features' within existing furnished holiday letting property.
- Buying property from friends or relatives and then adopting it as a furnished holiday let (the allowances will often be restricted to begin with but there will still be a continuing benefit).
- Adopting one of your own existing properties as a furnished holiday let (again, the allowances will initially be restricted but there will be a continuing benefit).
- Purchasing new furniture and equipment for furnished holiday letting property.
- Ceasing a furnished holiday letting business where the market value of the landlord's qualifying assets (on which capital allowances have been claimed) is less than the balance on the landlord's capital allowances pools.
- Starting a new furnished holiday letting business.

Chapter 5

Loss Relief

5.1   CURRENT BENEFITS

At present, losses arising in a furnished holiday letting business may be set off against the landlord's other income of the same tax year and the previous one.

Losses arising in 2008/9 or 2009/10 may also be carried back for set off against profits from the same business in the previous three years (with a £50,000 limit on losses arising in each year carried back more than a year).

This means that landlords with furnished holiday letting businesses making losses are currently able to reduce or eliminate their current tax bills under self-assessment, or obtain repayments of tax paid under PAYE or other tax paid at source.

Alternatively, furnished holiday letting landlords may carry their losses back to the previous year and obtain a repayment of tax paid then.

Furnished holiday letting landlords making losses in 2008/9 or 2009/10 may also be able to obtain repayments of up to £20,000 (£50,000 x 40%) in Income Tax paid on profits from the same business up to three years earlier.

This all adds up to the fact that a furnished holiday letting loss arising in 2009/10 can generate valuable tax repayments for almost any landlord with any taxable income in 2008/9 or 2009/10 or with furnished holiday letting profits in 2006/7 or 2007/8.

Capital Gains Tax Relief

Where the landlord has insufficient other income in either the current tax year or the previous one to utilise a furnished holiday letting loss, they may claim to set the excess off against any capital gains arising in the relevant year.

This should generally be regarded as a 'last resort', since the furnished holiday letting loss will then only produce a Capital Gains Tax saving at 18% rather than an Income Tax saving at up to 40% (or possibly even more if the loss is carried forward and set off against future rental income).

On the other hand, where there is no realistic prospect of utilising the loss in any other way in the foreseeable future, a claim to use it for Capital Gains Tax relief may perhaps be worthwhile.

5.2   FUTURE RESTRICTIONS

Under current rules, UK rental losses can only be set against UK rental profits and foreign rental losses can only be set against foreign rental profits.

Where the landlord has an overall net loss from all of their UK rental properties or all their foreign rental properties (as the case may be), that loss can only be carried forward for set off against future UK rental profits or future foreign rental profits (as the case may be).

Furnished holiday lettings are currently an exception to this rule, but this exception will cease to apply from 6th April 2010.

From 6th April 2010, losses from furnished holiday lettings will suffer the same restrictions as other rental losses and will only be eligible for set off against other UK rental income, or other overseas rental income, as the case may be. Only capital allowances will be eligible for set off against other income, as explained in Section 4.4.

There is therefore now a limited window of opportunity for furnished holiday letting landlords to obtain tax relief for any losses arising before 6th April 2010. After that, the scope for relief will be severely restricted.

5.3   THE ECONOMIC BACKGROUND

As we saw in Section 1.1, one of the qualifying conditions under the furnished holiday letting regime is that the furnished holiday letting business is carried out on a commercial basis, with a view to the realisation of profits.

This means that a business which consistently makes losses may not qualify under the furnished holiday letting regime.

However, with the UK currently wallowing in the depths of recession, many perfectly viable and 'commercial' furnished holiday letting businesses will be making losses during 2008/9 or 2009/10.

In other words, making a loss during 2008/9 or 2009/10 is not likely to threaten your business's qualifying status under the furnished holiday letting regime, as long as you have generally made profits in the past.

New furnished holiday letting businesses which commenced in the last couple of years will not have a history of making profits. These businesses may still make losses during 2008/9 or 2009/10 without threatening their qualifying status under the furnished holiday letting regime, as long as the landlord has a realistic expectation of making profits in the future.

In most cases, therefore, it can be regarded as perfectly reasonable for a furnished holiday letting business to make losses during 2008/9 or 2009/10 and still meet the qualifying conditions of the furnished holiday letting regime.

This opens up the opportunity for furnished holiday letting landlords to obtain tax repayments by taking suitable action to create or enhance losses arising in 2009/10 and, to a limited extent, 2008/9.

5.4   CREATING OR ENHANCING LOSSES

Let's get one thing straight. There is no point spending £100 just to get a tax repayment, or reduction, of £40 when you wouldn't otherwise have spent that money.

I am not for a moment suggesting that anyone deliberately wastes their hard-earned money just to create a loss for tax purposes. (If you're that obsessed with saving tax at any cost, I suggest you give the money to charity under Gift Aid instead.)

However, if you spend £100 now and get a tax repayment or reduction of £40 instead of spending money after 5th April 2010 and getting no tax relief, or only getting tax relief much later, then it is worthwhile.

In other words, it is the timing of your business expenditure which you should be looking at. How can you accelerate expenditure which you will be making anyway so that it creates or enhances a loss in 2009/10 for which you can get tax relief against your other income or against earlier furnished holiday letting profits as far back as 2006/7.

In the next few sections, we will look at some of the ways you can accelerate normal business expenditure in order to create or enhance a loss in 2009/10.

We will also look at some of the other things you might want to do, including the few cases where spending money just to save tax could be worthwhile: like paying your spouse or partner a salary.

Wealth Warning

Any furnished holiday letting losses arising in 2009/10 or earlier which are not set off against other income or capital gains arising in 2009/10 or earlier can only be carried forward for set off against future UK rental profits or future foreign rental profits (as the case may be).

Hence it will generally only be worth creating or enhancing your furnished holiday letting losses if you have other income, or previous profits, which you can set them against.

Wealth Warning 2

Accelerating expenditure to create or enhance a loss in 2009/10 may result in higher rental profits arising in 2010/11.

This is not a problem if your highest rate of Income Tax in 2010/11 is the same as, or lower than, in 2009/10, but may backfire if you have a higher marginal rate of Income Tax in 2010/11, such as when your total income in 2010/11 is between £100,000 and £112,950 or over £150,000, or if you are a basic rate taxpayer in 2009/10 but a higher rate taxpayer in 2010/11.

Quick reminder: Maximising your available capital allowances in 2009/10 is a good way to create or increase your furnished holiday letting losses. The methods set out in Section 4.12 are therefore equally relevant here.

5.5   ACCELERATING EXPENDITURE

As explained in the previous section, accelerating normal business expenditure may enable you to create or enhance a loss arising in 2009/10.

However, it is important to appreciate that this only applies to certain types of expenditure.

Paying your electricity bill early does not affect the timing of tax relief, as this is a 'continuous service' and must be accounted for in the period to which it relates.

In fact, paying any bill earlier does not help matters, as it is the date on which expenditure is incurred which determines when tax relief is due.

Expenditure is incurred as the cost arises. Hence, for example, an electricity bill covering the period from 6th January to 5th April 2010 is an allowable cost of the business for 2009/10 regardless of when the invoice is issued and regardless of when it is paid. Conversely, there is nothing you can do to make the bill for the period from 6th April to 5th July 2010 an allowable cost of 2009/10.

Hence, to accelerate business expenditure into 2009/10, you need to incur a cost by 5th April 2010 which you might otherwise have only incurred later.

Repairs and Maintenance

The best example of expenditure on which you can accelerate the timing of tax relief by incurring the expenditure earlier is repairs and maintenance.

Landlords with furnished holiday letting properties who carry out repairs, decorating and other maintenance work by 5th April 2010 will be able to claim the cost in their 2009/10 accounts.

Remember, you only need to carry out the work by 5th April 2010 (i.e. incur the expenditure); it does not matter when you pay the bill.

Advertising and Promotion

Another area where expenditure can be accelerated is advertising and promotion. If you run all your advertising for the 2010 season in March 2010, you will be able to claim the cost in 2009/10.

Remember that the advertising or promotion must actually take place by 5th April 2010, it is not sufficient merely to pay for it in advance.

Professional Fees

Many professional fees, such as legal fees and accountancy fees, are effectively for 'continuous services'. Like your electricity bill, there is therefore little you can do to control the timing of your tax relief.

If, however, you want to do something which is effectively a 'one-off', like renewing your rental agreements or your staff's employment contracts, doing this by 5th April 2010 will enable you to claim the cost in 2009/10.

Re-Financing

Re-mortgaging your furnished holiday letting properties during 2009/10 may increase your allowable interest costs. You will also be able to claim part (perhaps all) of any loan arrangement fees and associated professional costs.

See the Taxcafe.co.uk guide *'How to Avoid Property Tax'* for further details.

Things Not To Do

The best types of expenditure to accelerate are generally repairs and maintenance or 'one-off' intangible items like advertising or professional fees.

Continuous services and most 'tangible' expenditure cannot be accelerated effectively. If you were to buy a year's worth of toiletries and cleaning materials, for example, you would have to treat these as stock and only claim the cost when they were used.

5.6   SALARIES AND BONUSES

In Section 5.4, I pointed out that there is generally no point in incurring additional expenditure just to save tax.

The major exception to this is paying salaries to family members.

You can generally pay a salary of up to £110 per week or £476 per month to a spouse, partner or child aged 16 or over free from National Insurance.

You can generally also employ children aged 13 to 15 to do light work (e.g. paperwork or light cleaning), although there are restrictions on the hours which children of school age may work and some local authorities do not permit employment of 13-year olds.

Salaries paid to children aged under 16 are exempt from National Insurance.

Salaries paid to family members in 2009/10 will also be free from Income Tax as long as the recipient has no more than £6,475 of total taxable income (including the salary) during the year.

If the family member has total income between £6,475 and £43,875 in 2009/10, the salary will be subject to Income Tax at 20%. However, it could still be worthwhile paying the salary where you are paying Income Tax at 40% yourself.

You will obtain tax relief for salaries paid to family members, provided that:

- The amount paid is justified by the amount of work they do in your business.
- The salary is actually paid to the employee.
- The employee is free to keep the money themselves and there are no conditions requiring them to repay it to you.

Bonuses

Naturally, you will not generally wish to pay any non-family member employees any more than you normally would.

You can, however, accelerate the timing of relief for their pay by paying them a bonus in place of a later pay increase.

A bonus paid to employees will be an allowable cost for 2009/10 if:

i)   You have a commitment to pay the bonus and this commitment is in place by 5th April 2010 (e.g. you have written to the employees to advise them that they will be paid a bonus).

ii)   You actually pay the bonus by 5th January 2011.

Bonuses are subject to PAYE and employer's secondary National Insurance in the same way as regular pay but the employee may sometimes enjoy a primary Class 1 National Insurance saving.

5.7   ACCRUALS AND PROVISIONS

As explained in Section 5.5, the timing of relief for business expenditure depends on when that expenditure is incurred, not when it is paid for.

It is therefore important to ensure that all costs incurred up to 5th April 2010 are included in your 2009/10 accounts.

Where you have received an invoice by 5th April 2010, but have not yet paid, the item should be included as a creditor,

Where you have incurred the expenditure by 5th April 2010, but have not yet been invoiced, you need to make an accrual for the cost in your 2009/10 accounts.

Typical items to be accrued in a furnished holiday letting business's accounts include:

- Repairs and maintenance costs
- Utilities
- Telephone, fax and internet charges
- Bank charges and interest
- Wages for the period from the last pay date up to 5th April
- Legal and professional costs
- Accountancy fees (the costs of preparing your 2009/10 accounts and tax return should be included in your 2009/10 accounts)

Provisions

In exceptional cases, you may be able to include a provision for a future cost in your 2009/10 accounts.

A provision for a future cost will be an allowable cost in your 2009/10 accounts if:

i) The provision relates to a situation already in existence at 5th April 2010,
ii) You have a legal or contractual obligation to incur the expenditure, and
iii) The provision has been calculated on a reasonable scientific basis and represents a genuine quantification of the estimated cost – i.e. not just a pure guess.

Example

Trevor has several furnished holiday letting properties. In January 2010, he is subject to an electrical safety inspection and, in February, he receives a legal notice requiring him to rewire some of his properties.

In March 2010, Trevor gets a quotation for the rewiring work at £10,000. The work does not commence until May.

Although he has not actually incurred the expenditure during 2009/10, Trevor can include a £10,000 provision in respect of this work in his 2009/10 accounts.

Debtors and Stock

Debtors (amounts due from tenants) and stock (e.g. stationery, toiletries or cleaning materials) should be included as assets in the landlord's accounts.

This means that income is taxed as it arises and the cost of tangible items is only recognised as they are used (as explained in Section 5.5).

However, a provision can be made for any debts due which appear irrecoverable (bad debts) and for the cost of any stock which cannot be used.

Note also that debtors should only be included in the 2009/10 accounts where they relate to a rental period before 6th April 2010. A deposit due in respect of a booking for a period after 5th April 2010 should not be included.

2008/9

The principles set out in this section can also be applied when preparing your 2008/9 accounts. This provides the same opportunities to generate tax savings or repayments by creating or enhancing a loss.

Accruals and provisions made in 2008/9 will naturally lead to increased profits, or reduced losses, in 2009/10.

In some cases, however, a loss arising in 2008/9 may be better than a loss arising in 2009/10, although this depends very much on the precise circumstances of the individual landlord.

5.8   DEFERRING INCOME

A loss for 2009/10 could also conceivably be created or enhanced by deferring furnished holiday letting income until after 5th April 2010. In this regard it is important to remember that deposits received for bookings for periods after 5th April 2010 should not be included in your income in your 2009/10 accounts. This includes the latter part of any period spanning 5th April 2010.

Beyond this, however, there is very little you can do to defer furnished holiday letting income (without losing it altogether: which would be crazy).

But, if someone asks if they can book your property for either the week commencing 27th March 2010 or the week commencing 10th April 2010, you could perhaps consider telling them it is only available for the later week.

5.9   ACCELERATING OTHER INCOME OR GAINS

As explained in Section 5.4, to get relief for a furnished holiday letting loss arising in 2009/10, you will need to have income or capital gains to set it against.

In Section 5.1, we saw that there are many options for relieving a furnished holiday letting loss arising in 2009/10. However, if you still appear to have insufficient income to relieve the loss, you could consider accelerating some other type of income, such as:

- Paying yourself a dividend or salary out of a company you own (but beware of the National Insurance consequences of paying a salary).
- Deferring qualifying expenditure in any trading business which you own (by following the reverse of the strategies discussed in the last few sections).
- Disclaiming capital allowances due in any trading business which you own.

You should consider the full implications of any of these techniques, however, including their impact on your National Insurance liabilities or any Tax Credit claim.

As a last resort, you could consider realising capital gains by selling or transferring assets before 6th April 2010. This would give you scope to relieve your furnished holiday letting losses but, as explained in Section 5.1, the saving generated will be at just 18%, so this is generally only worth considering when all else fails and losses carried forward are unlikely to be relieved in the foreseeable future.

Chapter 6

Pension Contributions

6.1 THE CURRENT POSITION

Furnished holiday letting profits are currently eligible 'earnings' for pension contribution purposes.

Furnished holiday letting income is the only form of income which an individual can use to fund pension contributions, with full tax relief, without incurring National Insurance. (Although some furnished holiday letting landlords are paying Class 2 National Insurance at £2.40 per week.)

6.2 ACTION TO TAKE BY 5TH APRIL 2010

From 6th April 2010 furnished holiday letting profits will cease to be eligible 'earnings' for pension contribution purposes.

Thereafter, a landlord with no other earned income (i.e. salary or trading profits) will only be able to obtain tax relief on a maximum pension contribution of £3,600 per year (gross) – equivalent to a net contribution of £2,880.

Landlords with furnished holiday letting income may therefore wish to consider maximising pension contributions in 2009/10 in order to obtain full tax relief at up to 40% (or even effective rates of 42.5% in some cases).

Those with total income of £130,000 or more in 2009/10, 2008/9 or 2007/8 need to beware of the 'anti-forestalling' provisions if making total gross pension contributions of more than £20,000 during 2009/10.

All taxpayers are also subject to the annual allowance and the lifetime allowance (see Appendix A).

For further details on the maximum pension contributions eligible for tax relief see the Taxcafe.co.uk guide *'How to Save Tax 2010'*.

Chapter 7

Inheritance Tax

7.1 BUSINESS PROPERTY RELIEF

As explained in Section 1.2, some furnished holiday letting businesses are currently exempt from Inheritance Tax.

This is due to an Inheritance Tax exemption known as business property relief which provides 100% relief from Inheritance Tax for qualifying business property. (In some cases, the relief may be at just 50%, but this will not apply where the landlord owns the furnished holiday letting property personally.)

The current position is that a furnished holiday letting business may qualify for business property relief where the lettings are generally short-term and the owner (or their agents or employees) is substantially involved with the holidaymakers' activities.

This goes somewhat beyond the usual qualification requirements under the furnished holiday letting regime (see Section 1.1).

To be 'short-term' in this context, the lettings should generally be for no more than a fortnight.

Substantial involvement in the holidaymakers' activities is more difficult to quantify but would generally require some sort of physical presence at the site of the holiday accommodation. In other words, the owner, or their agents or employees, generally needs to be on hand to assist the tenants on a daily basis.

Even at the moment, therefore, the Inheritance Tax exemption for furnished holiday lettings is not widely available and it is difficult to know whether it will in fact actually apply in any individual case.

7.2   BUSINESS AS USUAL

The current Inheritance Tax treatment of furnished holiday letting businesses arises as a consequence of HM Revenue and Customs policy and not as a direct result of the furnished holiday letting regime.

Furthermore, HM Revenue and Customs has now specifically confirmed that the current position will remain unaltered following the abolition of the furnished holiday letting regime on 6th April 2010.

Hence, any furnished holiday letting business which currently qualifies for business property relief should continue to qualify after 5th April 2010.

The problem, as discussed in Section 7.1, is that it is not always clear which businesses qualify under the current rules!

What we do know is that, under basic principles, any business which does not consist wholly or mainly of making or holding investments should qualify for business property relief. This principle is what lies behind the current HM Revenue and Customs policy on this issue (did you think they were just being generous?)

Basically though, whilst it is 'business as usual' as far as business property relief on furnished holiday lettings is concerned, landlords generally still don't really know where they stand.

In the next section, I will therefore take a brief look at what planning can be done to shelter the value of furnished holiday letting properties from Inheritance Tax. More details on the planning techniques described in the next section can be found in the Taxcafe.co.uk guide *'How to Avoid Inheritance Tax'*.

7.3 SHELTERING THE VALUE OF A FURNISHED HOLIDAY LETTING BUSINESS

Landlords owning furnished holiday letting businesses can shelter the value of those businesses from Inheritance Tax in a number of ways, including:

- Gifting it to another individual and surviving seven years. This carries a risk that an Inheritance Tax charge will arise if the transferor dies within seven years, sometimes even when the property currently qualifies for business property relief. This risk can be covered by term assurance if desired.

- Selling it and reinvesting the proceeds in qualifying business property (see below).

- Selling it and reinvesting the proceeds in an Inheritance Tax shelter, such as a loan trust or discounted gift trust.

- Selling the business to a spouse or civil partner and using a 'family debt scheme' to shelter the proceeds by transferring an 'IOU' to children or other beneficiaries.

- Transferring the business into trust. The Inheritance Tax treatment of trusts is extremely complex and is discussed in detail in the Taxcafe.co.uk guide *'How to Avoid Inheritance Tax'*. Under the right circumstances, however, a trust can be an effective mechanism for sheltering assets from Inheritance Tax on the death of the transferor after more than seven years.

- Re-mortgaging the furnished holiday letting properties and investing the borrowed funds in qualifying AIM shares (see below) or another Inheritance Tax shelter such as a loan trust or discounted gift trust.

- Converting the business to a trading business (see Chapter 8).

Qualifying Business Property

Whilst the Inheritance Tax position for furnished holiday letting properties is somewhat doubtful, the position for other businesses is often more certain. Assets qualifying for business or agricultural property relief include:

- An interest in a trading business
- Shares in an unquoted trading company (including shares listed on the Alternative Investment Market - 'AIM')
- Agricultural property within the European Economic Area (see Appendix B)

('Trading' includes professions.)

A purchase of new qualifying assets generally provides exemption from Inheritance Tax after two years.

However, where a furnished holiday letting business which would have qualified for business property relief is sold and the proceeds are reinvested in qualifying replacement business property within three years, the replacement property generally provides immediate exemption.

The former furnished holiday letting landlord would, however, be exposed to an Inheritance Tax risk during the period between the disposal of the furnished holiday letting business and the acquisition of replacement property.

Nevertheless, this does provide an opportunity to move wealth from furnished holiday letting properties, where the Inheritance Tax position is doubtful, to other assets, where business property relief may be more certain, without running the risk that you might actually be giving up an existing entitlement to relief which you already have.

Chapter 8

Trading Status

8.1 GENERAL PRINCIPLES

As discussed in Section 2.2, there is a good chance that a small proportion of furnished holiday letting businesses could be treated as trading businesses under general principles.

I can recall staying in a self-catering cottage in South Wales a few years ago. The cottage was part of a small development with perhaps a dozen other similar properties. The complex also included a crazy golf course, a games room and an indoor swimming pool. The owner lived on site and was on hand to deal with any minor maintenance problems and to give advice on local tourist attractions.

I don't know for sure, but that landlord in South Wales may have been running a trade and I would argue that many furnished holiday letting businesses could also be trades under general principles.

Wherever the landlord provides a significant level of services in addition to the accommodation, there is an argument that a trading activity exists. The landlord does not have to provide these services personally, but could do so through agents or employees.

Just how many additional services are required is hard to say. It's a bit of a 'grey area', with no clear boundary between trading and mere rental income.

HM Revenue and Customs published some guidance on the subject on 9th December 2009. This made it clear that they are likely to put up strong resistance to any claims for trading status for a furnished holiday letting business. Even in the rare instances that they seem willing to accept that a trading activity is going on they want to treat it as a separate business to the property rental.

This, however, is merely HM Revenue and Customs' view and is not necessarily supported by the law. Parliamentary debates reported in Hansard in 1984 (when the furnished holiday letting regime was being introduced) make it clear that there is a significant degree of doubt over this issue. Even the Chief Secretary to the Treasury at the time expressed the view that some furnished holiday lettings might qualify as trades under general principles.

For 26 years, the matter has been left in abeyance as the furnished holiday letting regime effectively resolved the issue without anyone having to take a case to court.

Sadly, however, this now leaves us in a very unsatisfactory position, with no clear guidelines on when furnished holiday lettings should correctly be regarded as a trade under general principles.

Nevertheless, despite HM Revenue and Customs' view, it may be open to many furnished holiday letting landlords to claim trading treatment for their business after 5th April 2010.

8.2   BENEFITS AND COSTS

Establishing your furnished holiday letting business as a trading business will preserve most of the current advantages of the furnished holiday letting regime, but it will come at a cost: National Insurance.

Not just the Class 2 of £2.40 per week which some are already paying, but also Class 4 at 8% on income between £5,715 and £43,875 and at 1% on income over £43,875 (increasing to 9% and 2% respectively from 6th April 2011).

It is also worth remembering that whilst claiming trading treatment will mean retaining capital allowances, it also means forgoing the 10% wear and tear allowance, which could be more beneficial in some cases.

Any non-residents with a UK furnished holiday letting business also need to take care. Currently, they would generally be exempt from UK Capital Gains Tax on their furnished holiday letting properties, but they would usually be subject to UK Capital Gains Tax on any property which is part of a UK trading business.

Nevertheless, despite the few potential drawbacks, those with a good case for claiming trading treatment for their furnished holiday letting business from 6th April 2010 should consider whether such a claim might be beneficial.

8.3   ACHIEVING TRADING STATUS

Furnished holiday letting landlords whose position may currently be borderline could consider increasing the level of services provided to tenants in order to achieve trading status by 6th April 2010.

Each case will need to be considered on its own merits, but some of the appropriate steps which could be taken in some cases might include:

- Providing meals or refreshments
- Providing cleaning services or fresh linen during (not just between) tenants' occupation
- Providing games or other recreational facilities
- Living on-site to provide maintenance services and tourist information
- Opening an on-site shop

Chapter 9

Additional Points to Consider

9.1   ADOPTING A PROPERTY AS A FURNISHED HOLIDAY LET

Several of the tax planning measures described in this guide are dependent on adopting a property as a furnished holiday let before 6th April 2010.

The question we face, therefore, is how can a landlord adopt a newly acquired or existing property as a furnished holiday let in time, before the furnished holiday letting regime is abolished?

The current rules are that a newly acquired property, or an existing property which is being let furnished for the first time, must meet the qualifying conditions set out in Section 1.1 for the twelve month period commencing with the first letting (rather than for the tax year in which the first letting takes place) in order to qualify as a furnished holiday let from the date of that first letting.

Hence, under the current rules, in order to get a newly acquired property, an existing unfurnished rental property, or an existing unrented property (such as your own home) to qualify as a furnished holiday let before 6th April 2010, you will need to:

i)   Rent the property furnished for the first time before 6th April 2010,

ii)   Rent the property on a commercial basis with a view to the realisation of profits for a period of at least 12 months,

iii)   Make the property available for commercial letting to holidaymakers and tourists (i.e. the general public) for at least 140 days in the 12-month period commencing with the first furnished letting,

iv)   Actually let the property to holidaymakers and tourists (drawn from the general public) for at least 70 days during the 12-month period commencing with the first furnished letting, and

v)   Not let the property to the same person for more than 31 consecutive days at any time during a period of at least seven months out of the 12-month period commencing with the first furnished letting. This seven month period need not be a single continuous period but must include the lettings under (iv) above.

Technically, there only needs to be a furnished letting before 6th April 2010, although I would strongly advise making sure that you have an actual holiday letting before then.

Luckily, Easter Sunday falls on 4th April in 2010, making the week commencing 3rd April 2010 one of the most popular weeks for short breaks in the UK. Even a short letting for the Easter weekend will be enough to get your furnished holiday letting business started in time.

Example

Fred buys a cottage in Cornwall in February 2010 intending to use it as holiday accommodation.

In March 2010, he advertises the cottage for holiday rental. His first tenants rent the property for the week commencing 3rd April 2010.

The cottage will qualify as a furnished holiday let in 2009/10 provided that Fred:

i)   *Rents it out on a commercial basis for the year to 2nd April 2011,*

ii)   *Keeps it available for holiday lets until at least 21st August 2010, or for any other 140 day period during the year to 2nd April 2011,*

iii)   *Rents it to holidaymakers or tourists for at least 70 days during the year to 2nd April 2011, and*

iv)   *Does not rent it to anyone for more than 31 consecutive days during a period of at least seven months during the year to 2nd April 2011 which need not be continuous but must include the 70 days of rentals under (iii).*

Existing Furnished Rental Properties

It will be much harder to adopt an existing furnished residential rental property as a furnished holiday let before 6th April 2010, as the property will need to meet the qualifying conditions set out in Section 1.1 for the year ended 5th April 2010 (or the 12-month period commencing with the first furnished letting if this was after 6th April 2009).

9.2 STAMP DUTY LAND TAX

Stamp Duty Land Tax is currently payable on the total of the actual or deemed consideration paid for a residential property at the following rates:

Consideration	Rate Applying
Up to £125,000	Nil
£125,001 to £250,000	1%
£250,001 to £500,000	3%
Over £500,000	4%

The threshold above which the 1% rate begins to apply was temporarily increased to £175,000 from 3rd September 2008 to 31st December 2009 but was reduced back to its former level of £125,000 from 1st January 2010.

Actual consideration includes any amount payable for the property, even amounts left outstanding as a loan. It also includes the outstanding balance on any mortgage or other loan over the property for which liability is assumed by the transferee.

Example

Ford sells a furnished holiday letting property to his wife Anna for £20,000 subject to her also assuming responsibility for the outstanding mortgage of £160,000.

The total consideration is therefore £180,000 and Anna must pay Stamp Duty Land Tax of £1,800 (at 1%).

Transfers to a Company

For transfers to a connected company, the actual consideration paid is disregarded and Stamp Duty Land Tax is payable on deemed consideration equal to the property's market value.

Linked Transactions

Where two or more properties are acquired from the same transferor at the same time, or as part of a single contract or other arrangement, the rate of Stamp Duty Land Tax will be based on the total consideration, or deemed consideration, for all of the properties.

As we saw in Section 3.6, this is a particular problem for landlords transferring furnished holiday letting properties into a company.

9.3 THE PERILS OF PERSONAL USE

Any subsequent personal use of property by a transferor after a gift, sale at undervalue, or transfer to a connected company, should generally be avoided. Such use may give rise to one or more of the following:

- Personal Capital Gains Tax liabilities on a subsequent sale of the property
- Income Tax charges under the Pre-Owned Assets legislation
- Additional Inheritance Tax charges on a 'Gift with Reservation'
- Increased Corporation Tax charges
- Income Tax benefit in kind charges and Class 1A National Insurance costs
- Lost interest relief

Further information on these matters is provided in the Taxcafe.co.uk guides *'How to Avoid Inheritance Tax'* and *'Using a Property Company to Save Tax'*.

Chapter 10

Extension to the European Economic Area

10.1 RETROSPECTIVE EXTENSION

Prior to 22nd April 2009, the furnished holiday letting regime applied only to property situated in the UK.

However, under European Law, member states are prohibited from acting in any way which hinders the ability of European citizens to live, work or invest in any part of the European Union. As a consequence, the UK Government has now had to admit that restricting the furnished holiday letting regime to UK property only amounted to unfair discrimination and has been forced to extend the regime to property throughout the European Economic Area (see Appendix B).

Better still, the extension of the regime to property located anywhere within the European Economic Area has been given retrospective effect.

Whilst many people owning foreign property could benefit under the furnished holiday letting regime, it is important to realise that it is only available when the property meets all of the qualifying conditions set out in Section 1.1, including being let out on a commercial basis as a genuine profit-making venture. Most foreign holiday homes will not meet this criterion.

10.2 RELIEFS AVAILABLE

Qualifying property may be treated as if it qualified since it was first let as qualifying furnished holiday accommodation (or since the relevant country joined the European Economic Area, if later).

The relevant Capital Gains Tax reliefs, as set out in Chapter 3 (plus business asset taper relief on disposals which took place before 6th April 2008), can currently be claimed on transfers and disposals taking place as far back as 6th April 2003. The deadline for these claims depends on the tax year in which the relevant transaction took place, as follows:

Tax Year of Transaction	Claim Deadline
2003/4	31st January 2010
2004/5 and 2005/6	31st March 2010
2006/7	31st January 2011
2007/8	31st January 2012
2008/9	31st January 2013

Claims for capital allowances, or to set losses off against other income, must be made by amending the landlord's Tax Return. A special extension was given in respect of relevant amendments to 2007 Returns. Sadly, however, this extension expired on 31st July 2009, making the year to 5th April 2008 the earliest period which may currently still be amended, with the usual deadline of 31st January 2010 applying.

Amended Income Tax claims are not permitted in respect of earlier periods, which are now out of date for amendment under self-assessment. This arises under the usual UK tax rule which precludes such claims when returns were submitted in accordance with the law as it was then understood. This may possibly be contrary to European Law, so it could be worth considering making provisional claims.

10.3 CAPITAL ALLOWANCES

Capital allowances can generally be claimed on qualifying assets (see Section 4.1) still in use in the foreign furnished holiday letting property at the beginning of the relevant tax return period (e.g. assets in use on 6th April 2007 for a 2008 Tax Return).

Claims should be based on the purchase price of assets bought on or after the date the property is treated as having first qualified (or 1st January 1994, if later). Assets already in use in the property on this date (or 1st January 1994, if later) should be brought into account at their market value on this date.

Example

Joe has a villa in Malta which now qualifies as a furnished holiday let. Joe bought the villa in 2002 but, as Malta only joined the European Union on 1ˢᵗ May 2004, the villa can only qualify from this date.

Joe spent £10,000 furnishing the villa in 2003. On 1ˢᵗ May 2004, the villa's existing furnishings had a market value of £7,000. In March 2007, Joe bought a new television for the villa at a cost of £2,000 and, in May of the same year, he spent £5,000 on new kitchen equipment.

Joe can submit an amended tax return for the year ended 5ᵗʰ April 2008 at any time up to 31ˢᵗ January 2010. He will be able to claim writing down allowances at 25%* on the £7,000 market value of the furnishings already in place on 1ˢᵗ May 2004, plus the £2,000 cost of the television bought in March 2007, as these items were in use in the villa on 6ᵗʰ April 2007, at the beginning of the return period.

Joe will also be able to claim writing down allowances at 25%* on the kitchen equipment bought in May 2007 (this is before the annual investment allowance was introduced in April 2008 and is also based on HM Revenue and Customs' view that first year allowances are not available on assets within rental properties - see Section 4.2).

* - Writing down allowances on the general pool were given at the rate of 25% prior to 6ᵗʰ April 2008.

If Joe misses the 31ˢᵗ January 2010 deadline for amending his 2008 Tax Return, he can still claim capital allowances on the same assets in his 2009 Tax Return, provided that they were still in use in the property at 6ᵗʰ April 2008. The rate of writing down allowances he can claim will, however, be reduced to just 20%.

10.4   ALL OR NOTHING

There are some potential drawbacks to claiming furnished holiday letting treatment for a foreign property. As explained in Section 1.3, neither the 10% wear and tear allowance nor the landlords' energy saving allowance is available on furnished holiday letting property.

Furnished holiday letting treatment does not have to be claimed on a qualifying property outside the UK but, if you do claim, you must make all of the appropriate adjustments. So look before you leap!

10.5   TAX RETURNS AND LOSS RELIEF

The treatment of losses arising from furnished holiday lettings outside the UK but within the European Economic Area is a little confused. HM Revenue and Customs has issued instructions suggesting that this income should be included in the UK property pages of the tax return. This means that any losses arising will automatically be set off against any UK rental income which the individual has, with any surplus being available for set off against their other income. Losses arising during 2008/9 or 2009/10 may again also be carried back up to three years, as explained in Section 5.1.

Strictly speaking, however, any overseas furnished holiday lettings are still part of an individual's overseas letting business and any losses arising should really be set against any other overseas property income which they have in priority to anything else.

In practice, this will seldom make any difference to the individual's overall tax position but, if you feel that HM Revenue and Customs' rather makeshift solution to dealing with furnished holiday lettings outside the UK is putting you at a disadvantage, you should argue for the strict correct treatment to be followed.

Appendix A

UK Tax Rates and Allowances: 2008/9 to 2010/11

	Rates	Bands, allowances, etc.		
		2008/9	2009/10	2010/11
		£	£	£
Income Tax				
Personal allowance		6,035	6,475	6,475
Basic rate band	20%	34,800	37,400	37,400
Higher rate/Threshold	40%	40,835	43,875	43,875
Personal allowance withdrawal				
Effective rate/From	60%	n/a	n/a	100,000
To		n/a	n/a	112,950
Super tax rate/Threshold	50%	n/a	n/a	150,000

Starting rate band applying to interest and other savings income only

	10%	2,320	2,440	2,440

National Insurance Contributions

Class 1 – Primary	11%	) On earnings between earnings threshold and		
Class 4	8%	) upper earnings limit		
Earnings threshold		5,435	5,715	5,715
Upper earnings limit		40,040	43,875	43,875
Class 1 – Secondary	12.8%	- On earnings above earnings threshold		
Class 1 & Class 4	1%	- On earnings above upper earnings limit		
Class 2 – per week		2.30	2.40	2.40
Small earnings exception		4,825	5,075	5,075
Class 3 – per week		8.10	12.05	12.05

Pension Contributions

Annual allowance	235,000	245,000	255,000
Lifetime allowance	1.65M	1.75M	1.8M

Capital Gains Tax

Annual exemption:			
Individuals	9,600	10,100	10,100(1)
Trusts	4,800	5,050	5,050(1)

Inheritance Tax

Nil Rate Band	312,000	325,000	325,000
Annual Exemption	3,000	3,000	3,000

Pensioners, etc.

Age allowance: 65-74	9,030	9,490	9,490
Age allowance: 75 and over	9,180	9,640	9,640
MCA: born before 6/4/1935 (2)	6,625	6,965	6,965
MCA minimum	2,540	2,670	2,670
Income limit	21,800	22,900	22,900
Blind Person's Allowance	1,800	1,890	1,890

Notes
1. The annual exemption for 2010/11 has not yet been announced but appears likely to remain at the current level.
2. The Married Couples Allowance, 'MCA', is given at a rate of 10%. A lower allowance of £6,535 applied in 2008/9 where both of the couple were aged under 75 throughout the year.

The European Union &
The European Economic Area

The European Union

The 27 member states of the European Union are:

Austria	admitted 1st January 1995
Belgium	founding member
Bulgaria	admitted 1st January 2007
Cyprus	admitted 1st May 2004
Czech Republic	admitted 1st May 2004
Denmark	admitted 1st January 1973
Estonia	admitted 1st May 2004
Finland	admitted 1st January 1995
France	founding member
Germany	founding member
Greece	admitted 1st January 1981
Hungary	admitted 1st May 2004
Irish Republic	admitted 1st January 1973
Italy	founding member
Latvia	admitted 1st May 2004
Lithuania	admitted 1st May 2004
Luxembourg	founding member
Malta	admitted 1st May 2004
Netherlands	founding member
Poland	admitted 1st May 2004
Portugal	admitted 1st January 1986
Romania	admitted 1st January 2007
Slovakia	admitted 1st May 2004
Slovenia	admitted 1st May 2004
Spain	admitted 1st January 1986
Sweden	admitted 1st January 1995
United Kingdom	admitted 1st January 1973

Any rights which citizens of countries admitted on 1st May 2004 or 1st January 2007 have under UK tax law commence on the date that their country was admitted to membership.

The European Economic Area comprises the 27 member states of the European Union plus Iceland, Liechtenstein and Norway.

Appendix C

Connected Persons

The definition of 'connected persons' differs slightly form one area of UK tax law to another. Generally, however, connected persons include the following:

- Husband, wife or civil partner
- Mother, father or remoter ancestor
- Son, daughter or remoter descendant
- Brother or sister
- Mother-in-law, father-in-law, son-in-law, daughter-in-law, brother-in-law or sister-in-law
- Business partners
- Companies under the control of the other party to the transaction or of any of his/her relatives as above
- Trusts where the other party to the transaction, or any of his/her relatives as above, is a beneficiary

Pay Less Tax!

...with help from Taxcafe's unique tax guides and software

All products available online at **www.taxcafe.co.uk/books**

How to Avoid Property Tax
By Carl Bayley BSc ACA

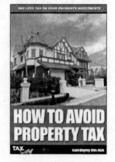

How to Avoid Property Tax is widely regarded as *the* tax bible for property investors. This unique and bestselling guide is jam packed with ideas that will save you thousands in income tax and capital gains tax.

"A valuable guide to the tax issues facing buy-to-let investors" - THE INDEPENDENT

How Tax-Free Property Investments
By Nick Braun PhD

This guide shows you how to double your investment returns using a variety of powerful tax shelters. You'll discover how to buy property at a 40% discount, paid for by the taxman, never pay tax on your property profits again and invest tax free in overseas property.

Using a Property Company to Save Tax
By Carl Bayley BSc ACA

This guide shows how you can significantly boost your after-tax returns by setting up your own property company and explains ALL the tax consequences of property company ownership.

How to Avoid Tax on Foreign Property
By Carl Bayley BSc ACA

Find out everything you need to know about paying less tax on overseas property. Completely up to date with key UK and overseas tax changes.

Property Capital Gains Tax Calculator
By Carl Bayley BSc ACA

This powerful piece of software will calculate in seconds the capital gains tax payable when you sell a property and help you cut the tax bill. It provides tax planning tips based on your personal circumstances and a concise summary and detailed breakdown of all calculations.

Non-Resident & Offshore Tax Planning
By Lee Hadnum LLB ACA CTA

By becoming non-resident or moving your assets offshore it is possible to cut your tax bill to zero. This guide explains what you have to do and all the traps to avoid. Also contains detailed info on using offshore trusts and companies.

The World's Best Tax Havens
By Lee Hadnum LLB ACA CTA

This book provides a fascinating insight into the glamorous world of tax havens and how you can use them to cut your taxes to zero and safeguard your financial freedom.

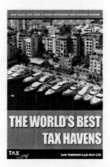

Tax Saving Tactics for Non-Doms
By Lee Hadnum LLB ACA CTA

This unique tax saving guide explains in plain English the new tax rules for non-domiciled individuals that allow you to keep money offshore and tax free.

Using a Company to Save Tax
By Lee Hadnum LLB ACA CTA

By running your business through a limited company you stand to save tens of thousands of pounds in tax and national insurance every year. This tax guide tells you everything you need to know about the tax benefits of incorporation.

Salary versus Dividends
By Carl Bayley BSc ACA

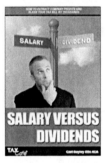

This unique guide is essential reading for anyone running their business as a limited company. After reading it, you will know the most tax efficient way in which to extract funds from your company, and save thousands in tax!

Keeping It Simple
By James Smith BSc ACA

This plain-English guide tells you everything you need to know about small business bookkeeping, accounting, tax returns and VAT.

Selling Your Business
By Lee Hadnum LLB ACA CTA

This guide tells you everything you need to know about paying less tax and maximizing your profits when you sell your business. It is essential reading for anyone selling a company or sole trader business.

How to Avoid Inheritance Tax
By Carl Bayley BSc ACA

Making sure you adequately plan for inheritance tax could save you literally hundreds of thousands of pounds. *How to Avoid Inheritance Tax* is a unique guide which will tell you all you need to know about sheltering your family's money from the taxman. This guide is essential reading for parents, grandparents and adult children.

The Investor's Tax Bible
By Lee Hadnum LLB ACA CTA

This tax guide can only be described as THE definitive tax-saving resource for stock market investors and traders. Anyone who owns shares, unit trusts, ISAs, corporate bonds or other financial assets should read it as it contains a huge amount of unique tax planning information.

Disclaimer

1. Please note that this Tax Guide is intended as general guidance only for individual readers and does NOT constitute accountancy, tax, investment or other professional advice. Neither Taxcafe UK Limited nor the author can accept any responsibility or liability for loss which may arise from reliance on information contained in this Tax Guide.

2. Please note that tax legislation, the law and practices by government and regulatory authorities (e.g. HM Revenue and Customs) are constantly changing. We therefore recommend that for accountancy, tax, investment or other professional advice, you consult a suitably qualified accountant, tax specialist, independent financial adviser, or other professional adviser. Please also note that your personal circumstances may vary from the general examples given in this Tax Guide and your professional adviser will be able to give specific advice based on your personal circumstances.

3. This Tax Guide covers UK taxation only and any references to 'tax' or 'taxation' in this Tax Guide, unless the contrary is expressly stated, refer to UK taxation only. Please note that references to the 'UK' do not include the Channel Islands or the Isle of Man. Foreign tax implications are beyond the scope of this Tax Guide.

4. Whilst in an effort to be helpful, this Tax Guide may refer to general guidance on matters other than UK taxation, Taxcafe UK Limited and the author are not expert in these matters and do not accept any responsibility or liability for loss which may arise from reliance on such information contained in this Tax Guide.

5. Please note that Taxcafe UK Limited has relied wholly on the expertise of the author in the preparation of the content of this Tax Guide. The author is not an employee of Taxcafe UK Limited but has been selected by Taxcafe UK Limited using reasonable care and skill to write the content of this Tax Guide.

Lightning Source UK Ltd.
Milton Keynes UK
26 January 2010

149115UK00001B/117/P